Jean-Pierre and Luc Dardenne

Contemporary Film Directors

Edited by James Naremore

The Contemporary Film Directors series provides concise, well-written introductions to directors from around the world and from every level of the film industry. Its chief aims are to broaden our awareness of important artists, to give serious critical attention to their work, and to illustrate the variety and vitality of contemporary cinema. Contributors to the series include an array of internationally respected critics and academics. Each volume contains an incisive critical commentary, an informative interview with the director, and a detailed filmography.

A list of books in the series appears at the end of this book.

Jean-Pierre and Luc Dardenne

Joseph Mai

UNIVERSITY OF ILLINOIS PRESS
URBANA
CHICAGO
SPRINGFIELD

Manufactured in the United States of America
1 2 3 4 5 C P 5 4 3 2 1
This book is printed on acid-free paper.
Frontispiece: Jean-Pierre and Luc Dardenne on the set. © Christine Plenus

Library of Congress Cataloging-in-Publication Data
Mai, Joseph.
Jean-Pierre and Luc Dardenne / by Joseph Mai.
p. cm. — (Contemporary film directors)
Includes bibliographical references and index.
ISBN 978-0-252-03528-9 (cloth : alk. paper) —
ISBN 978-0-252-07711-1 (pbk. : alk. paper)
1. Dardenne, Jean-Pierre, 1951—Criticism and interpretation.
2. Dardenne, Luc, 1954—Criticism and interpretation.
I. Title.
PN1998.3.D364M35 2010
791.4302'330922—dc22 2009030034

Contents

Preface and Acknowledgments | ix

ENCOUNTERS THROUGH A FRAME | 1

Militant Video 1

The Workers' Movement 10

Words and History 15

Flashes of Hope 20

Falsch (1987) 24

Against Speed 30

Punching the Clock: *Thinking of You* (1992) 33

Behind Our Images: A New Beginning 40

La Promesse 44

A Sensuous Realism 53

Budget and Rhythm 63

Rosetta and Émilie Dequenne 65

The Son 82

The Rhythm of Tears: *The Child* 101

Dans l'Obscurité 117

Postscript: *Le Silence de Lorna* 118

INTERVIEW WITH JEAN-PIERRE AND LUC DARDENNE | 125
Filmography | 141
Bibliography | 147
Index | 153

Preface and Acknowledgments

I would like to make a film that is also a handshake.
—Luc Dardenne, *Au dos de nos images,* 10

"A film that is also a handshake": This transsensorial metaphor—mixing vision, touch, affect, and ethics—is worth unpacking as one approaches the cinema of Jean-Pierre and Luc Dardenne. *La promesse* (1996), the film that brought the Belgian-born brothers to worldwide recognition, gives an idea of what a cinematic handshake might resemble. As the credits roll, we do not get the music and creative graphics that usually transition us into a world of fiction. Instead there are simple red credits over a black screen, telling us the mundane funding sources of the film, including the Belgian lottery, and a "foundation for social action." There is no mention of actors, only the directors' quick signature and the title. We are bathed in everyday sounds, recorded directly: the low hum and clicking of a gas pump, the slam of a car door, simple sounds that transition the viewer not into a fictional world, but into the everyday world that awaits us every time we step outside. The Dardennes' films are not so much understood on a symbolic level, through characters, decors, and lighting, as felt on a tactile or emotional level.

La promesse follows the struggles of Assita, an undocumented Burkinabe immigrant in Belgium. In several scenes she carries a boxy shopping bag with thick vertical stripes of red, white, and blue. It is made of cheap, fibrous nylon, can be bought at discount stores, and is meant to be disposable. Like Assita, who carries everything she owns in it, the bag is resilient. But its function is not metaphorical. This concentration on detail and the long sequence shots throughout the film give the bag a tactile quality, at least in my personal experience of the film, for I can feel its distinct fibrous texture between my fingers. It remains in my mind long after viewing as well, orienting my attention to other such bags that I have seen, often carried by other immigrants like Assita, in the urban markets of France. This bag is furthermore but one small example of the tendency to evoke touch in this film; *La promesse* and other Dardenne works are filled with weights, shapes, textures, and smells that evoke our senses and that can lead us to draw complex, and sometimes highly individualized, associations.[1] There is a strong transcendent element to viewing these objects and bodies, which we do not passively observe from the comfort of our seats through a frame that separates us from the film's world.

It is tempting to simply explore the richness of all these textures. But the film's style is not aiming at a sensuous experience situated entirely outside the realm of concepts and reasoned thinking. The handshake metaphor is not only tactile—it also reveals a generous appeal to the viewers' sense of solidarity with others. *La promesse* doesn't separate us from daily life in the way many adventure or war films do, but actually leaves us with a heightened awareness of our place within a broader context. The film gives us a diachronous experience: We become sensitized to the dramatic situations, but through various stylistic means—including a suddenly stationary camera at film's end—the film reminds us that it is but light and shadow and that any new sensibility the film has given us must take hold in our own world where we make our own decisions. Permeated by the social problems of the global economy—with its closed factories, rampant unemployment, and clandestine immigration—the Dardennes' work becomes critical by teaching us to relate in a physical way, to be sensitive to bodies and objects that we may normally ignore or overlook. The historian Arlette Farge has observed that the Dardennes' work has a strong tendency to "incarnate history," and "captures in movement the experience of being in the world at a given moment" (Farge 2008, 134, 136). The point of their cinema is not to relay the viewer into an imaginary world, but to teach him or her to perceive better than before in order to readjust our views and behavior.

This book will attempt to describe and interpret the Dardennes' style through a chronological treatment. The Dardennes' search for a film-as-handshake has led them on a winding aesthetic journey in search of a proper style that has now become recognizably "Dardennian." Looking over a career spanning more than thirty years and including numerous documentary and fiction periods, one detects a major stylistic shift beginning with their first widely acknowledged film, *La promesse.* In their early phase as documentary makers, style, as it was for many politically minded filmmakers in the post-1968 context, seems to have been a tool for exploring the crossroads of history, politics, and personal identity. In these low-budget and rather militant films made throughout the seventies and early eighties, the brothers sought to give voice to the marginalized working class of the city they had known since childhood, Seraing, Belgium. Through complex and highly self-conscious stylistic techniques—playful montage, long tracking shots, purely symbolic images, and a lyrical and probing voiceover—they attempted to interpret their subjects' lives in this desolate environment. During these years the brothers developed many of the themes and aesthetic concerns that have remained with them, but, to anyone encountering these documentaries after the brothers' later films, they will have little in common stylistically.

In their earliest forays into fictional cinema, style was again a mediation through which the brothers explored the thickness of history as it is imposed on individual subjectivities. The first of these, *Falsch* (1986), is a self-conscious experiment in narrative juxtaposition, exploring the weight of the past on Joe, the last survivor of a family that has perished in the Holocaust. The action is set in a dark, empty airport where Joe encounters his family's ghosts; past and present are jumbled together, imprisoning Joe in an antinaturalistic *mise-en-scène* filled with haunting off-screen voices. Their second fictional film was one the brothers considered a failure, *Thinking of You* (1992), a socially aware romantic drama that works through conventional stylistic devices to portray the psychological effects of unemployment, a theme dear to the brothers. This mainstream film, with a sizable budget, recounts a father's descent into solitude through emotive music, moody lighting, expressive clothing and makeup, and especially the classical performances of its professional actors.

Many of these early films are successful in what they do. But in all of them, whether they are conventional or experimental, documentary or fiction, formal mediations tend to explore in an analytical manner the psychological effects of history on individuals. At times they leave the viewer, and, to hear the Dardennes tell it, even the directors, feeling on the outside looking in. We sit in the movie house or in front of the television screen and we understand the characters, but we are no more engaged with them than in many other types of cinema. Worse, the brothers felt that *Thinking of You* gave an insipid version of their cherished themes precisely because their artistic control had been taken away by the overbearing and conventional practices of the film industry. Discouraged, the brothers reevaluated the type of cinema they wanted to make, coming to a radical conclusion recorded in Luc's journal-form book, published as *Au dos de nos images* [On the Back of Our Images], to which I refer throughout this book. It is there that Luc formulates his above-mentioned desire for film as handshake, and also there that he traces his and Jean-Pierre's rejection of almost all aspects of mainstream filmmaking in its financing, casting, direction, and aesthetics.

The work that resulted was *La promesse,* which arrived at Cannes and on the international circuit with a bang. From this moment on, the brothers have left behind both the highly mediated experimentations of *Falsch* and the conventional compositions of *Thinking of You.* Their films are now neither self-consciously "art-house" nor conventionally consumable. Dropping the extradiegetic music, voiceovers, and self-conscious montage of *Falsch,* the brothers intensify the viewers' experience with long sequence shots, rhythmic movements, an extremely edgy handheld camera, and abrupt editing. The stylistic changes from *Thinking of You* are perhaps most obvious in the brothers' use of actors. They would now as gladly show us their actors' hands or the backs of their heads as a portrait of their faces. Their characters are now psychologically absent from the viewer, their motivations are mysterious, and at times characters undergo major ethical or psychological transformations without the viewer having the slightest clue of what has happened. Nor is the lack of psychological motivation compensated by a tightly woven narrative, for major events occur in ellipses (or off screen), in an editing style that eschews causality and that will be described often in this book. Instead, the brothers film actors as physical bodies—weights and shapes, voices and hands—coming into various forms of contact with each other: touching, facing, weighing, measuring, striking, carrying, and crying together, often with the rhythm and variation of ballet. As in the title of Luc's journal, the camera remains "behind" things, without a synoptic view, dragging us into the action of the shot. Abstract categories that were essential to their previous work—class, nation, gender, race—remain relevant, but they do not define a frame that we observe. The frame no longer surrounds and encloses characters but is determined by their encounters and indicates a continuation of space beyond, a space that leads directly to our own world.

This style has underpinnings in the Dardennes' broad intellectual culture. (*Au dos de nos images* cites a wide range of philosophers and literary artists.) In this culture, it is perhaps the ethics-first philosophy of Emmanuel Levinas that resonates best with the worlds of their films. Playing on Sartre's famous existentialist precept from *L'existentialisme est un humanisme*—"existence precedes essence"—Levinas begins his philosophical endeavor from the point of view that "ethics precedes existence." For Levinas, ego-based theories of subjectivity fail to account for the basic fact that people are born into social relations with others before they acquire any power of decision, relations they have not chosen, but to which they are ultimately responsible. According to Levinas, we are not cogs in a "totality" that we can somehow master or even perceive from the outside; instead we are always already involved in an "infinite" and noncircumscribable web of encounters. This requires us to respond (or refuse to respond, a response in itself) to the others whose faces and demands ceaselessly confront and beseech us. Experience is considered first and foremost in points of contact, and in the Dardennes' films these most often take the form of neglect or violence, or, on the contrary, of the solidarity implied in the handshake. Some of the most moving scenes in their work—Igor's promise to Hamidou and Assita, Roger's refusal to help, Rosetta's humiliation at the end of *Rosetta,* Bruno's acceptance of responsibility in *The Child,* and so forth—are focused on characters who turn toward others, often with a discovery of shame or guilt, at times with tears, and realize that they are not alone. The Dardennes' films often end at a beginning—at the awakening to a relationship whose development is left open to the viewer's imagination.[2] Throughout, I will be exploring this varied ethical landscape.

Another, but related, intellectual influence over the Dardennes has been their religious culture. Like most children of their generation growing up in French-speaking Wallonia, the brothers attended a Catholic grade school where they became familiar with religious stories and the Catholic-Left moral system. Religion for the Dardennes, however, is not much connected to doctrine, or even to faith in God. In ways similar to Levinas, who often referred to the relation between self and other as one of transcendence of the self in a religious bond, a "re-ligio" (playing on the perhaps fictional etymological sense of religion as a "linking together"), the Dardennes redefine religion in terms of a social transcendence. Many of their films can be understood as secular rewritings of religious stories and themes. *Falsch,* for example, transposes the story of Jacob and Joseph to the post-Holocaust memories of a New York Jew. I will read Olivier and Francis's trip to a deserted lumberyard in *The Son* in part through its resemblance to the story of Abraham and Isaac venturing to the mount where the sacrifice is to be made. When Bruno cries in *The Child,* he extends a long sacred tradition of tears and their moral import. Igor's promise and sacrifice, Rosetta's shame, Francis's guilt, all these themes and many others partake of an ongoing transposition of religious traditions in a nonreligious, completely social context.

This ethics of relation is not merely a theme of the films, but provides a framework for the Dardennes' working method, another recurring theme in this book. Christine Plenus's beautiful photo of the brothers working on the set of *The Child,* which serves as frontispiece to this book, captures an analogous turn away from directorial "control" toward collaboration and mutual commitment. In their working methods, these "bicephal" filmmakers (as they call themselves) hardly evoke the "prestige of the individual" that poststructuralists like Roland Barthes condemned when they killed off the author (Barthes, 50). As in the photo, there is no strict creative center, no authoritative voice in the Dardennes' work. They flourish in an atmosphere where people—usually actors and crews with whom they have worked on multiple films—are not merely doing a job, but developing trust and making demands upon each other in a shared project. It is a process without outside financial constraints, which the brothers have jealously protected by self-producing all their films since *Thinking of You.*

Reminiscent of this photo, and somewhat paradoxical in a book called *Jean-Pierre and Luc Dardenne,* it is far from my intentions to paint a psychological portrait of the brothers, though I will provide many details about their origins, the development of their working methods, and their intellectual interests. Just as the brothers avoid a synoptic view, I feel compelled to jump inside the encounter with the film to accept their extended hand and take stock of how it feels. Even the very important political contexts of their films will at times be left, not unacknowledged, but momentarily off screen like so much of the Dardennes' film world. First describing the elements of style, we can then venture out toward the realities the films address with a deeper perception and with more compassion for the people involved. Indeed, the Dardennes films might be considered empathy-producing machines. In other words, the forms that the Dardennes searched for so long and hard draw the viewer into the same ethical place from which the films were conceived.

It is true that many viewers may be socially and culturally "constructed" not to answer to this appeal. Despite the cachet of multiple awards at Cannes and other festivals around the world, their films seem destined to remain "minor," made outside industrial circuits. And the Dardennes do not necessarily make it easy for an audience to appreciate them. A handshake is a sign of love, but it is not always gentle. Sometimes it feels more like a shove, as their hyperactive camera and abrupt cuts induce headaches, turn stomachs, or momentarily break our grip over the images we are watching. It is perhaps one of the brothers' most courageous and critical moves that they are willing to remain indifferent to the box office in order to shake their viewers out of complacency. For they are not interested in making films viewers love, just films that love their viewers. For many, a film by the Dardennes is a transformative experience: "Maybe that is the mirror of the art of cinema. . . . To perceive in the night of the cinematic projection the other that is yourself and that your daily life occults" (L. Dardenne 2008, 58). The Dardennes' cinema is neither a form of entertainment nor a denunciation, but an act of love, the ethical love for a society in which people are interrelated:

> "If you loved me, you would have changed me." This is the response from a spectator to a film that has not succeeded in loving him or her. Love the spectator to the point of setting in motion his or her desire, opening him or her up to the time of the film. . . . One might answer that the love of the film for the spectator is impossible since the spectator is socially and culturally constructed to not receive this address. But someone has to start. It's our role to begin, even if failure is more probable than success. (L. Dardenne 2008, 13)

| | |

I am grateful to many colleagues and friends whose help has been essential to the completion of this book. James Quandt of the *Cinémathèque Ontario* was extremely generous early in the project in helping me access the Dardennes' documentaries. Sarah Cooper and Martin O'Shaughnessy commented on the ideas that formed the seed of the book. At my home institution, Clemson University, Mike Lemahieu, Todd May, Elizabeth Rivlin, Aga Skorobka-Bates, and Susanna Ashton provided vital feedback on the manuscript or the ideas that went into it. Diane Perpich helped me develop an understanding of and appreciation for Levinas's philosophy. I would also like to thank the College of Arts, Architecture, and Humanities and the Department of Languages of Clemson University for teaching release and financial support while I was working on the project.

In Belgium I would like to thank Les Films du Fleuve and especially Delphine Tomson for her help in choosing set photos and stills from the Dardennes' earlier films. Christine Plenus was extremely generous in granting permission to publish her set photos. I am also grateful to Gabrielle Claes for her assistance at the *Cinémathèque Royale Belge*. Very sincere thanks go to Marc-Emmanuel Mélon and his colleagues of the University of Liège for welcoming me and scouting Seraing with me, and without whom I would not have met many wonderful community members who have worked with the Dardennes. I would also like to give a big "merci" to Jean-Pierre for graciously spending a morning discussing his work with me.

Parts of the argument about *La promesse* have been reworked from an article I published in *Esprit Créateur*, edited by Martin Crowley. The interview with the Dardennes first appeared in *Cahiers du cinéma* in October 1999, and was conducted by Bernard Benoliel and Serge Toubiana.

My final gratitude goes to Tatjana Mai-Wyss for being a perceptive and committed partner throughout this project.

Notes

1. A second example is even more personal. Assita carries an object that has always had an astounding effect on me; a religious statuette she has brought from Burkina Faso. We see it with Assita, then broken in two by some bikers,

and finally repaired by a boy, Igor, who is trying to help her. After the statuette is broken, she wraps its head in a white handkerchief. This head, wrapped in this way, has always reminded me of an object from my own past, working in a factory in an American rust-belt city during the late 1980s, a memory reinforced by the presence in the film of many similar objects, sounds, even the suggestion of the smell of oil that I glean from the garage where Igor works. The statuette's head has a certain weight, size, and form that remind me, strangely enough, of a mango that one worker, a Jamaican, often wrapped in a cloth and placed on his workbench. Previously unconscious elements of the past come to mind: the transcultural mixture (and conflicts) of the Polish, Hispanic, rural, urban, white, and African-American workers.

2. I am by no means the first to point out the link between the Dardennes and Levinas's philosophy, the first of course being the Dardennes themselves. My work has especially benefitted from the fine analyses of Sarah Cooper (2007). See also O'Shaughnessy (2008) and Cummings (2008).

Encounters Through a Frame

Militant Video

When *La promesse* was revealed at the Cannes festival in 1996, it was hailed as a startlingly original breakthrough film. Audiences particularly noted its stark but hopeful depiction of Seraing, the disaffected suburb of Liège, where the Dardenne brothers filmed. It is, however, still surprising to some viewers that *La promesse* was not the Dardennes' first attempt to film this space, nor even their second, but that they had been making documentary films about Seraing and its inhabitants since the early 1970s. In fact, their undying devotion to the place is probably unique among filmmakers and endures to the present day, even if they have set their most recent film, *Le silence de Lorna* (2008), 10 kilometers away in Liège.

They started small, with "documentaires d'intervention"—unedited militant works shown in schools, workers' lodges, and housing complexes—and then moved to more polished television documentaries before finally turning to straight fiction filmmaking in the early 1990s. As Luc Dardenne has explained, one must be careful to see in the documentaries and the first fictions a straight line leading to *La promesse* (Dardenne 1996–97, 7). Yet a consideration of the Dardennes' documentary career gives an understanding of both the brothers' strong sense of solidarity with this community and their immense efforts, with paltry means, to bring its concerns and problems to a wider audience. Furthermore, in the details of these films one can detect the seeds of the Dardennes' later, affective cinema.

Jean-Pierre and Luc Dardenne were born (1951 and 1954 respectively) in the French-speaking Belgian town of Engis, along the river Meuse, a small town that owes its modest renown to pollution and paleontology. Most recently Engis is noted for its pollution emergencies, caused by the emissions of steel furnaces in the neighboring cities, especially Seraing (where the brothers attended school) and Ougrée, the most densely industrialized suburbs of Liège. But Engis has a long history as well, which the Dardennes, to my knowledge, have not mentioned: It was in Engis, in 1830, that the paleontologist Philippe-Charles Schmerling discovered skulls, the earliest that are now accepted as belonging to Neanderthal humans. There is something appropriate about this double heritage, for at times in the Dardennes' work it seems as if the Industrial Revolution and the primal struggle for shelter and reproduction of the Stone Age have more points of convergence than differences.

Early in the nineteenth century, the combination of the nearby coal beds and the navigable Meuse attracted many industrialists to the region. The river, central to the Dardennes' films even if it is not always shown, descends from the Ardennes in France toward the northwest, eventually crossing through this "sillon industriel" with Seraing on its Right Bank and most of Liège a few kilometers further on its Left Bank, before turning toward Maastricht and the Netherlands. Seraing owes its development to the arrival of John Cockerill, an English entrepreneur who effected the transition from charcoal furnaces to coke-burning blast furnaces, improving the efficiency of the steel production process and founding an empire. Belgium and the region of Liège, its skyline dotted with towering furnaces and billowing smoke even today, became European leaders of the Industrial Revolution. The majority of the inhabitants of Seraing—with such street names as rue de l'Industrie and rue Cockerill—and its outlying area have been employed by the steelworks since that time. The château that Cockerill bought from the prince-bishops of Liège continues to dominate the lower part of Seraing today, though its façade is now hidden from view by elevated multilane highways.

The Dardennes' work originated in the thriving working-class culture of Seraing and the other towns in the shadow of the Cockerill, Sambre, and Ougrée furnaces. Generation after generation, children have followed their parents into the factories, the churches, the unions, and the various societies that prepare for the Carnival celebration each year. The region's history includes heroes and major events, including some painful battles in World War I and a strong Resistance effort in World War II, perhaps none more important than the massive, but ultimately failed, general strike of winter 1960–1961, an important site of memory for Wallonians generally and the Dardennes in particular.

According to one plausible interpretation, the strike was related to the attempt of the European powers to retain their colonial possessions. The Congo, Belgium's lone colony, struggled for and won independence in 1960. A year earlier, anticipating the loss of this enormous source of wealth, the government was already preparing an austerity plan. The resulting revolts in Wallonia came from a widespread skepticism that Belgium's economic straits were indeed so strongly related to the Congolese situation rather than to corporate mismanagement and greed (Deprez 1963, 23). The miners of the Borinage region, whose chronic impoverishment had been the subject of the 1932 classic documentary *Misère au Borinage* by Henri Storck and Joris Ivens, were the first to strike, in 1959. In November 1960 the government proposed the infamous Single Law (*loi unique*) that significantly raised taxes while decreasing, without consultation, pension and unemployment benefits. The general strike came quickly after. It is almost an understatement to write, as do Neuville and Yerna, that "the Belgian working class has not only shown a great combativeness . . . but also a surprising capacity for self-discipline" (Neuville and Yerna 1990, 109). The strike, led by new public figures such as the communist André Renard, came furious and organized, especially in the region of Liège. Revolution filled the air. The Dardennes were just children at the time, but they have formative memories of public spaces transformed into mass social spaces with worker assemblies during this mythical event (see Mosley 2002, 165).

The workers' pugnacity did not make the strike a success. After some violent confrontations—occupations of train stations, clouds of teargas, threats to abandon work altogether—new elections were finally called, and the strike ended, against the wishes of many who invested their hopes in revolution. Newspapers of all political stripes declared victory, the single law was passed, people returned to their jobs embittered and disillusioned. The split between the more militant Wallonia and the more prosperous Flanders only grew, worsening the already contentious divide between the two main ethnolinguistic groups of the country. Perhaps most frustrating for the people of Seraing is that daily life saw scant improvement and has even gotten worse: Today unemployment in Wallonia reaches 17 percent, three times that of Flanders, and 27 percent in Seraing itself (Stroobants 2000). The city's social life has been deeply scarred. Driving through it today one sees block after block of half-inhabited rowhouses, industrial buildings in disuse, graffiti, prostitutes, and adolescents wandering through the streets.

Whenever the Dardennes tell stories of their youth, they describe events and people firmly rooted in local topography. They have given some of their most interesting interviews in Seraing, where the spaces loosen the brothers' rather restrained tongues. They tell stories of depressed workers killing themselves in the Meuse that they themselves feared, soccer games interrupted when pollution became so thick that they could not see the ball, and the strange characters who inhabited their neighborhood. There are fewer stories about the brothers themselves or their own family, a reticence owing to their private nature, and perhaps to the fact that their father stuck out from the local community as a white-collar employee of one of the companies. Later this state of things represented a slight disconnect between the Dardennes and their film subjects, as if they were watching everything from close by, but "through a window" (Dardenne 2008). The brothers' early films are inspired by their wish to discover more about those people and to help them formulate their own desires and demands in a nearly hopeless context.

One of the most important influences in their childhood was the Catholic grade school they attended in Seraing. The Saint-Martin school was surrounded by abandoned lots only a few meters from the Meuse. According to the Dardennes, the children in their grade school had the impression that the "factories were watching us," and they were forbidden from opening windows because the pollution would turn their writing paper brown (Waintrop 2003a). Catholic education has always been the rule in Belgium, and the Saint-Martin school was run by a left-leaning priest in the tradition of Seraing's working-class clergy. Though the brothers do not seem to have been particularly devout, they assimilated the stories of the Bible, traces of which can be found throughout their films. Their passion for the cinema was also stoked at the school, where one of the French professors, another priest, would transform a chapel into a cinema, screening heady films by the likes of Jean-Luc Godard, François Truffaut, and Bernardo Bertolucci. Here they also discovered Robert Bresson's *Mouchette* and *Au hasard Balthazar*, to which they pay homage on several occasions.

When the brothers left Seraing for the university in the early seventies, they did not have a specific vocation. Luc studied philosophy at the University of Louvain. Jean-Pierre pursued the theater, another passion indulged by the brothers in a *Serésien* cultural center, and one whose traces can be found in some of the brothers' most complex *mises-en-scène* (Teflin 2005). Taking up drama at the Institute for Performing Arts (Institut National Supérieur des Arts du Spectacle) in Brussels, Jean-Pierre met a theater director who would be instrumental in the brothers' artistic and political life: Armand Gatti.

Gatti was a dynamic and picaresque figure. Born in a Monegasque shantytown to an anarchist street cleaner and a Catholic mother, he left school at eleven (his father had died from wounds suffered during a strike) and worked odd jobs, including a stint as a gravedigger, another in a seminary, before joining the French Resistance and enduring internment in a German prison camp. He later befriended the Belgian poet Henri Michaux, and became an important playwright who also made a few underappreciated, but very strong, films. Influenced by both Jean Vilar's National Popular theater through the fifties and the more radical atmosphere of parallel thinking that dominated the stage of the late sixties, Gatti intended to democratize the theater, make it historically conscious, and break down the metaphorical wall between actor and spectator (Knowles 1989, 14–15). His work was eventually censored, notably with the cancellation of *The Passion of General Franco As Told by the Emigrants Themselves* at Vilar's *Théâtre national populaire,* due to pressure personally exerted on Charles de Gaulle by the Spanish dictator. After the play's cancellation in 1973, Gatti left France for Belgium.

In Brussels, Jean-Pierre, joined by Luc who became an assistant director, worked with Gatti on two productions, *La Colonne Durutti* and *L'arche d'Adelin,* both illustrations of Gatti's outlandish method. During vicious interrogations in the Nazi camp, Gatti had responded by improvising variations on poems as a resource from which he derived inner strength. He called this kind of poetic resistance "la parole errante," or the "wandering word," which speaks without answering. Gatti's conception of poetry is in some ways very traditional, for it allowed him to build an invisible, almost magical, shield against the forces of death in the world (Gatti 1997). At the same time, building on the Saussurian notion of *parole* as an individual use of language, he emphasized the individual subject against a political coercion that would silence the individual or make him or her say only what served power. Gatti sought to make the wandering word politically effective by organizing theatrical events in or about situations of political oppression, often in prisons and asylums, but asking the inmates themselves to have a hand in creation and performance.

Such concerns were, of course, in the air in a post-1968 France that included the situationists as well as filmmakers such as Marin Karmitz or Jean-Luc Godard. Alison Smith points to a number of themes that obsessed post-1968 filmmakers throughout the seventies, including the "destruction of the hierarchical structures of society" and a utopian foundation of a new one, the desire for a "*prise de la parole.*" The starting point of *La Colonne Durutti*—about the life of Buenaventura Durutti, an anarchist killed during the Spanish Civil War—was not a written text to be acted out, but a collective development of scenes of Durutti's life molded to the space in which it was presented. Researched and written by the students, the result was performed in an abandoned factory that was renovated with water and electricity. Because the space could not easily accommodate both actors and audience in any single room, the "play" (really a continuation of rehearsals) was performed among the audience members. Through participation it was hoped that stronger communities would take hold and speak with their own voice.

The Dardennes' second theatrical collaboration with Gatti, *L'arche de l'Adelin,* pushes the baroque logic of Gatti's theater to its limit. It has been called a survey play, a type of play developed by theater students going to the homes of schoolchildren, agricultural workers, and other groups, and asking them to write about various subjects (Knowles 1989, 208). *L'arche de l'Adelin* combines several of these projects, which collectively tell the story of Omer Labarre, a small landowner whose property is expropriated and who leads his flock of sheep to France. The giant "happening" included scenes from all of Labarre's life, using conventional theater but also puppets and video, and took place, simultaneously, on 145 tractor trailers driven from village to village in Wallonia. Many who gathered to watch this "play without spectators" had participated in its creation. In a continuum with the wandering word, Gatti called his poetics the "théâtre éclaté," and in addition to breaking down the border between writer, performer, and audience, his works would present characters from different time periods on a single stage, or the same characters at different stages of their lives, in a way that evokes "all possible pasts and futures, and conditionals of the present" in what he finally termed "l'écriture du possible" ("the writing of the possible" [Knowles 1989, 13]). *L'arche de l'Adelin* gave people a chance to speak in their own names, from their own spaces, in a manner that explores alternative social possibilities.

It was on projects such as these that the brothers first came into contact with video, using it as a tool to meet community members who would participate in the theatrical works. Gatti had asked them, for example, to locate and interview on video an immigrant from Eastern Europe, an anarchist who had left Belgium to fight in Spain. The method pleased them more than they thought it would, and when Gatti left Belgium to work in Germany, the brothers decided to spend a few months on the construction site of the Tihange nuclear plant, where they made enough money to buy a cheap Sony Portapak. One might call this the first example of their self-production. When they returned to Liège, they had no intention of becoming filmmakers or even any knowledge of filmmaking techniques other than what they had picked up from the autodidact Gatti; they simply found the medium easy to use and its "rapidity of intervention" useful to their pursuit of social action. Filmmaking was seen as a practical means of pursuing a larger, "on-the-ground militantism" (Frodon 1996, n.p.). Starting with a political desire, the brothers themselves slowly "wandered" into filmmaking from the outside.

Beginning in 1974, and continuing over the next few years, the brothers formed a video workshop that they revealingly called "Collectif Dérives," which had absolutely no legal status or recognition. The word *dérives* again refers to "wandering," or drifting, the meandering of a river, the Meuse, but it also evokes more post-1968 libertarian thought—the brothers have said that they took the concept from the Situationist International group. If so, it should be noted that drifting in their sense comes from an opposite direction from the Situationists' more famous notion of *détournement,* which involved tearing objects dear to bourgeois order out of their context and putting them to other, subversive ends. *Dérives* is a way *into* the city, flowing, meandering from the margins to the center. It involves forming a collective identity in the alienated margins of society and gradually bringing its concerns toward the center, causing a drifting of social hierarchies. Dérives is centripetal, not centrifugal, akin to the notion of *autogestion,* or "self-management," in industrial labor relations.

Like others who worked in social video at the time, the Dardennes saw the medium as a block for building a new culture. Their first films included short social "documentaires d'animation" or "documentaires d'intervention." As Luc has explained, "in the Estates, we filmed people's lives so that they would get to know each other better, so that they wouldn't remain in ignorance of each other despite their proximity" (quoted in Waintrop 2003b, 2). In Gattiesque fashion, the new and inexpensive form of communication could be used by the disenfranchised of their region to formulate desires and demands (see Dubois and Mélon 1991 for a history of video art in Belgium).

In a 1977 unpublished twelve-hour interview given to a student intern with *Dérives* named René Begon, when the brothers were 22 and 26 respectively, the Dardennes describe and judge their early video work at a moment when they were transitioning to more polished documentaries. Begon, who turned his interview into an undergraduate thesis, describes a fascinating project from 1974 that seems typical of this early period. Funded with a grant from a "Maison de culture" (a second self-production), the project employed video to encounter inhabitants of the Fagnes project, a complex housing workers in the upper part of Engis (situated higher on the hills moving up from the Meuse), and which had a bad reputation among the more middle-class residents of "lower

Engis" where, for example, the brothers' family resided. Dérives contacted several inhabitants—children, cleaning women, retired people, and so on—and interviewed them about their living space, filming in sequences, since editing equipment was too costly. After a couple of months, however, video was eclipsed. Because the younger inhabitants of upper Engis formulated the desire to have their own space, the group worked toward procuring an old house in the neighborhood. There was also a creative workshop for children on the theme of "creating an imaginary city" (Begon 1977, 44). The groups created a rather intriguing moving sculpture called the "beast of the flow" (again the river) and other marionettes made from garbage dumped in the area. Everything was shown at the community house. The work, which exacerbated some of the tensions in the housing complex, was not much appreciated by local politicians, and the grant was not renewed. The local groups certainly gained a voice, and hidden tensions were brought to the surface.

The Dardennes undertook many such projects during this period. The videos they made were never edited, sometimes were never seen, and often were made for one showing and erased afterward. They were not concerned with art or archiving, but with representation and creating a consciousness. They made films about the occupation of a foundry by its workers; another about a village school, shown to half the village. Many of the films trace the formation of a social space or the importance of possessing a space (especially for adolescents), the conflicts between generations, education, and the lives of immigrants. In terms of ideology they were almost anarchistic, geared toward understanding social reality rather than defending institutional lines: "it was a way of getting out of political language understood as a face-to-face between a revolutionary theory and a reality needing to be transformed. Video was a manner of approaching social reality more profoundly, to the extent that we were coming into contact with people, discussing their way of life, their questions, their worries, what they were doing, how they did them, how they saw their relation to society" (Luc quoted by Begon 1977, 38).

The brothers, however, were not satisfied with the use of video, which was often abandoned in favor of more concrete action. And yet, they found themselves more and more drawn to the complexities of filmmaking itself, and toward the possibilities of using the medium to bring the lives of the marginal to a larger audience. If they wanted to explore this interest further, they needed to change their approach. They would now propose a more precise film project, with research, and invite their subjects to participate in a more polished piece. The new concern for the product grew out of the centripetal logic of Dérives—more finished work could be shown on the television, and it could come into the homes of Belgians who would never make it to Seraing.

The Workers' Movement

These conclusions seem to have come, furthermore, at a time when the *video d'animation* itself had attained an artistic limit. For Marc-Emmanuel Mélon, the Dardennes mark the transition from video as *prise de parole* to its *mise-en-scène* (Dubois and Mélon 1991). Indeed, they quickly became the Belgian expression—among the most accomplished "reference points"—of a thriving worldwide video documentary culture, particularly strong in Belgium (Dubois 2006, 16). In part they were able to reach a larger audience due to the graces of Paul Tréfois and his television program *Vidéographies*, which broadcast for many years the work of experimental and social video artists from Europe and the United States. We should not exaggerate the professionalism of these works, however. Though the films were more polished, they were not made with great financial resources, and though copies exist, they are not easily seen outside of retrospectives of the Dardennes' work. Little has been published on them in English, save Martin O'Shaughnessy's perceptive analyses.

Dérives was also growing by increments. In 1975 the collective became an officially recognized nonprofit organization and won a subsidy from the Ministry of Culture, that was the equivalent of one person's salary for a year (Begon 1977, 66). The grant was to fund a project called "The History of the Workers' Movement in the Region of Liège from 1936 to Today." As the title indicates, this work would be informed by historical reflection and research in archives and through interview. The project was originally conceived to examine the meaning of political militancy after the great strike of 1960, but it was then enlarged to include workers' resistance in the Spanish Civil War and the occupation of Belgium during World War II. Three films that directly grew out of this project were completed: the now lost *Chant du rossignol (Song of the Nightingale*, 1978), *Lorsque le bateau de Léon M descendit la Meuse pour la première fois* (*When Léon M's Boat Descended the Meuse for the First Time*, 1979) and *Pour que la guerre s'achève, les murs devaient s'écrouler* (*For the War to Be Finished the Walls Must Have Fallen*, 1981), also called *Le journal*. Obviously, these films are made in a different temporal perspective from the militant documentaries, for they deal consciously with the past, though not as classic reconstructions or reenactments. Often they treat their archival sources with irony. Instead, they look at the past through memory, the memory of those who participated in events, and the effect of those events on their present lives.

Both *Léon M* and *Le journal* reconsider the great strike of 1960. Both of the films' main characters, Léon M. (whose last name was Masy) and Edmond, participated actively in the strike, and their recollections correspond remarkably, down to the very language they use to describe it. Masy, a burly, cigar-chewing, bare-chested figure, reminisces about the "truly unequaled feeling of fraternity" he experienced during the enormous street demonstrations. Edmond, who edited a clandestine newspaper titled the *Worker's Voice*, tells of "a truly new spirit" and "the most exalted years of our lives, when we were really alive." A soft-spoken but proud man, Edmond recounts with pleasure his role in the strike while we hear, with gentle irony, the *Communist International* playing in the background.

But this nostalgia appears only briefly, for the films seek not to dwell on the past but on its meaning for the present. In *Léon M* the Dardennes follow Masy, two decades after the strike, down the Meuse through Seraing and other factory communities, through what Jean-Marie Piemme has called a nature "that seems to have signed a pact with the devil" (Piemme 1996–97, 7). (See figure 1.) The film is structured by movement forward and backward as Leon's boat moves toward the future and his mind remembers the past. Léon no longer works in the Cockerill plant, but he seems to have work encoded in his genetic makeup: we first see him welding and hammering away at a metal boat that he has fashioned out of some rusting metal. As we ride with Léon down the Meuse, he points out places on shore where he and his companions gathered to march or do battle with the police. Interspersed with images of the boat, the film contains interviews on shore in which participants of 1960–61 revisit strike sites: women who blockaded the post office, men, masked

Figure 1. Early images of the Meuse. © Films du Fleuve

twenty years later, who describe their activities as railroad saboteurs. The interview technique imposes a montage that both links and separates the individual: Each interviewee is alone, living through memories. Fraternity has become solitude and we never see Léon with the others. The narrative proceeds like a mosaic of separate voices rather than an analysis of individuals caught up in an unfolding historical drama. The river alone organizes the film, but through sheer geographical chance and inexorable movement forward.

The element that would have transformed these disparate reflections into a coherent, heroic narrative is summed up in the word *utopia,* the same utopia that drove the brothers' work with Gatti and informed the "wandering word." Utopia was the historical motor behind the strikers' fraternal quest for revolution, the ultimate cause of what should have been a chain of reactions leading to its realization; but utopia finally eludes them. As Masy lumbers down the Meuse, a poetic and increasingly frantic voiceover describes his hesitation between the two symbols of the gull and the river. The gull embodies the future, progress, the promise of the sea, and the perfect society that the revolution hoped to produce. The reflection of the sky on the windshield of the motorboat serves as a constant reminder of this promise. But the river now passes through a rubble-strewn environment haunted by "the phantoms of a failed revolution." Near the end of the film, over an image of the tombstone of a dead marcher, a voice laments this "land of those who chase shadows." The tension of gull and river, idealism and rubble, is perhaps best captured in the Dardennes' montage and camera movement: Howling wind dominates the soundtrack while the bouncing images of the boat and its buoys alternate with archival images of the strike and shots from the Cockerill furnace. In these first of many images of the Meuse to be found in the Dardennes' films, the rhythm is not so much flowing as it is chaotic. As in Walter Benjamin's description of Paul Klee's *Angelus Novus,* progress, "a storm . . . blowing from Paradise," pushes the angel toward the future, but the angel would rather turn back toward the past to "awaken the dead, and make whole what has been smashed" (Benjamin 1969, 257–58). The past here lies in fragments that disrupt the present.

Like *Léon M., Le journal* focuses on space and Edmond's relation to the pockmarked geography of Seraing. While evoking his memories, Edmond walks the streets of Seraing, showing us the walls of the factories. In one scene the brothers accompany him on his Sunday walk in the hills overlooking Seraing. Here an establishing shot, during which Edmond points out the various factories and furnaces, reflects the voiceover description of Seraing in *Léon M.:* an "industrial passage won over by weeds, a sky striped with smoke, and smokestack totems." Even the pastoral landscape is made of scrap: the hills are actually slag heaps, or enormous piles of tailings from the mine that vegetation has grown over. These hills now surround Liège and its suburbs, and they will be found in later films as well. With their camera, the Dardennes take an ecological view, excavating the city's objects and spaces with techniques ranging from shoulder-held examinations of the nooks and crannies of disused factories to long tracking shots along their walls. Walls, those that would have had to fall in order for the war to end, sprawl endlessly. Sounds of dripping water combine with images of broken glass and crumbling brick reminiscent of Rossellini's *Germany Year Zero,* a film that Luc Dardenne has called a "model" for their later films. According to the voiceover, Seraing has become a "tragicomic" setting where human experience is now merely "part of the history of industrial archeology." Wild species of flora and fauna have sprung up in the abandoned factories: weeds cover the rubble (the landscape is notably bereft of trees), a feral cat leads the camera around an abandoned depot.

Human culture barely exists in such an environment. The "Worker's Voice," Edmond informs us, was not only concerned with political action, but with all aspects of the lives of workers, including leisure, art, and songs. But the new forms of culture never materialized. The camera follows Edmond as he wanders alone about the city, often in long shots that show him dwarfed by the factories (figure 2). Though passing automobiles and factory walls are all around, the spaces are empty of humans themselves. Edmond's home life is equally solitary: At home he sits alone at a table, the same table where the newspaper editorial staff used to huddle to write articles and plan demonstrations. We only briefly glimpse him with his son or his faithful dog, never with his wife. The film ends on a hauntingly melancholic note: Edmond drinks his coffee alone, listening to his radio. In a slow sequence he walks to his car, which sits alone in the middle of a parking lot, and drives away for another day of wandering. Human life has been desocialized, turned into a compulsive routine. All Edmond can do is walk around the factory

Figure 2. The walls that should have fallen.
© Films du Fleuve

walls, a postindustrial Jericho, and wait for a new voice that will make the walls tumble. At the end of the film, the camera remains fixed on the image of an empty street arched with a grass-covered overpass, nature slowly reclaiming the physical world. The film circles of Liège say that Edmond would later die alone and homeless.

Stylistically, *Léon M.* and *Le journal* cut across the grain of what one might expect from militant video. Spoken in voiceover by Luc Dardenne, the first words of the lost video *Song of the Nightingale* set the lyrical tone for these films: "Suspended between the walls of yesterday's citadel and today's city, the song of their resistance, like the Song of the Nightingale seeking a new land of repose, soars over the territory of our memory" (quoted by Aubenas 2005, 47). Both Leon and Edmond of *Le journal* are lyrical wanderers, dreamers whose actions and thoughts meander, independently of unions or political parties. Even the rubble-laden images have at times a rugged beauty. The voiceover interpellates history through poetry rather than theory (Aubenas 2005, 52). The camera bounces over the waves of the Meuse, is engulfed in the flames of the steelworks, or lingers on the animal life, the cat or the gulls. It is up to the viewer to decide whether this mediation succeeds in bridging the distance between Léon or Edmond and each one's situation.

Words and History

In 1981 the Dardennes renewed their collaboration with Gatti to assist during the filming of *Nous étions tous des noms d'arbre* (*We were all names of trees*, 1982). This audacious film returned the Dardennes to Gatti's baroque and collaborative working methods. It was made in a community workshop in Derry, Northern Ireland, during the hunger strikes of 1981 (shooting began on May 5, the day Bobby Sands died). Gatti chose to refer only obliquely to the strikes while remaining focused on the community workshop. He ties together numerous narrative strands: the salvaging of an old canon from a Spanish galleon, the death of a British soldier who rescued a Catholic family from a fire, the assassination of another British soldier, the video surveillance of the workshop, the death of two teenagers driving a florist's truck filled with explosives, and the roots narrative of an Irish American teacher. In each of these strands, the film brings into focus the relation between past and present, ideology and experience. Most of the roles are played by members of the workshop, especially Paddy Doherty, a Catholic who founded it. Doherty proposes debates about political events in which Catholics must take on the perspective of Protestants and vice versa.

Again language and voicing play an important role. The kids spray paint on everything, compose rock songs, take part in debates, and enact political situations. Gatti has explained that every one of his characters is inspired by a tree that he has encountered during his walks through the countryside near his home in the Italian Piedmont. These trees, which he also finds scattered in the writings of Leonardo da Vinci, suggest for him the idea of "verticality," of unfettered development toward self-realization. In the film, Doherty explains the history of the name Londonderry: In fact, the original Irish name of the city was Derry, which means, in Gaelic, "oak." He also points out that the names of all the characters in the old ogham alphabet used in Gaelic were names of trees. Imposed by the British colonizer, "Londonderry" renders the name meaningless. Gatti's aesthetics seem oriented toward creating the possibility for people to cultivate an authentic and lyrical nature—associated with the natural world—by furnishing them with a platform for using language creatively and reveal the true sense of words hidden under the palimpsest of colonialism.

Just after this collaboration, the Dardennes made, with help from Gatti's son Stéphane, a documentary that takes up the same themes, though in a more pessimistic mode. *R . . . ne répond plus* opens on a solitary young man repairing a radio control board. He tells a kind of parable, presumably to the camera, about a man who, standing on a beach, puts pebbles into his mouth and speaks into the wind. The cracking pebbles, the wind, and the voice evoke the sound of the radio, and *R . . . ne répond plus* will take for its subject the Radio Free movement of early 1980s Europe. The radio voice not only is a poetic sound (upon which the soundtrack plays enormously) but conveys a political truth: "politics is first and foremost a question of voice; radio is a question of voice," says the repairman, the man at the beach speaks against the din of the sea. The film follows several contributors to the Radio Free movement as they give voice to the antinuclear movement, student protests in Italy, local linguistic conflicts, and problems of racism encountered by immigrants. Voices heard on the radio here intervene into politics before rigid ideology can gain a foothold.

Over the radio waves flow voices without metadiscourses, or as one of the news producers at the radio station says, Radio Free "communicates facts without opinions," leaving the listener to come to his or her own conclusions. This is of course its strength. The Radio Free movement seems to realize Berthold Brecht's desire that the radio become a form of communication rather than distribution, that it "let the listener speak as well as hear . . . to bring him into a relationship instead of isolating him" (Brecht 1964, 52).

But the film's style cannot help revealing dissatisfaction with the radio as pure technology of communication, a dissatisfaction that may signify a deeper dissatisfaction with unfettered voicing, and a move away from some of Gatti's idealism. The viewer may quickly lose interest in a phone-in debate over who is the greater singer, Jacques Brel or Julio Iglesias (much of which is heard humorously over images of a deserted soccer field). The swirling cacophony of radio voiceovers that flood the end of the film testifies to the difficulty of "R," or "reality," to broadcast itself—R no longer answers. In some ways the film ends on the same malfunction ("nothing happens") that bothered the Dardennes in their early videos, as if the price of a free voice is a continual repairing of the soundboard. The free flow of language can be liberating, but without a project voices can become mere disconnected words (figure 3). Rather than invading the city from its margins, these voices are lost in the din of the sea.

Near the end of *Le journal,* Edmond illustrates the crushed hopes of his strike with a game of chess: First the pawns are taken; then more valuable pieces abandon the board; the queen; and finally, the game is over. The group of short, 7–10-minute films that compose *Leçons d'une université volante* (*Lessons from a Floating University,* 1982) teaches *its* lesson on a larger game board: a Europe divided by communism. The film's title refers to the clandestine "floating universities"—again evoking the meandering of the river—that pop up in private homes during moments of oppression of free expression in Polish history, including the period of Solidarity in the 1980s. These five separate vignettes were meant to float into the homes of Belgians, onto their television screen,

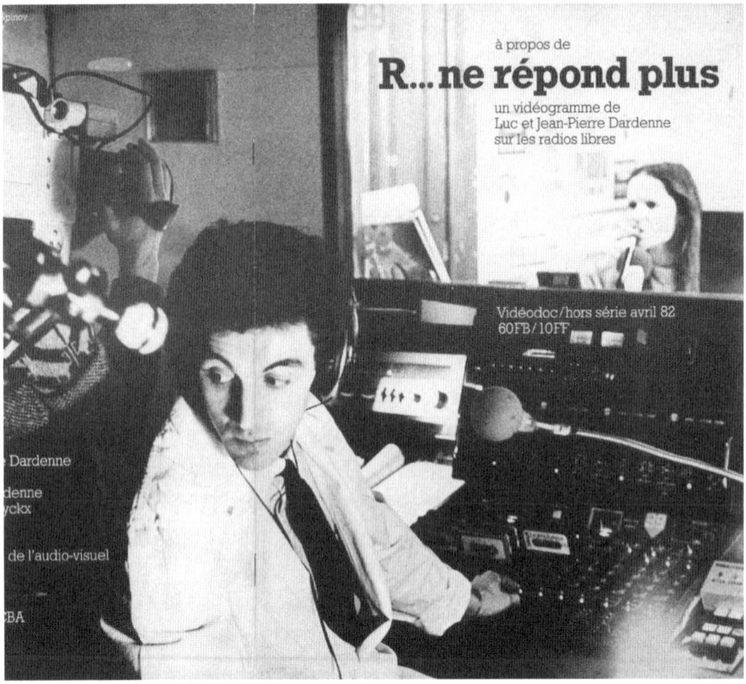

Figure 3. Disconnected voices. © Films du Fleuve

just before or after other programs and between commercial breaks. Their desire is to teach about forced immigration, and thus they playfully adopt the convention of a school lesson to tell the story of several Polish emigrants to Liège.

The pretext of the lesson is the train, the mode of transportation that brought all these people out of Poland. The train is also the exact opposite of the meandering river, for it follows its rails in one direction, from past to future, from East to West. At the beginning of each episode, a photo of a locomotive lies on a table while a voiceover explains: "This is a locomotive. In the words of Lenin, it is the locomotive of the revolution." A hand tosses photos of Stalin, Khrushchev, and Brezhnev onto the train: "three subsequent engineers." Then a picture of the locomotive transformed into a "war tank": Budapest, Prague, Warsaw. We then see a map of Eastern Europe, showing the path of the locomotive, and a map of Poland; finally a picture of the "new great engineer,"

Polish president Wojciech Jaruzelski (figure 4). The pedagogical voice is direct and unambiguous.

These lessons of official history are quickly undermined, however, by real lives and real voices that have experienced this train, voices provided by the Dardennes' camera. Again the brothers pursue parallel narratives: two generations of a family who react to news of the rising Solidarity movement; a young Jewish man, chased, along with his mother, from his home in 1968 by communist anti-Semites; a former resistance fighter and officer in the Polish peasant party and the editor of its newspaper; a man who teaches Polish songs to expatriates in Belgium. The film pursues two regimes of language use, one ideological, one experiential. In one vignette the family, listening to a Polish government radio broadcast around the kitchen table, shows off its skills at decoding official signifiers such as "free pricing standards" and "ideological supporters" into their actual signifieds, "prices imposed by the government" and "Solidarity members." These conversations do not teach in the direct way. Indeed, the distinctive narrative threads of the *Lessons* are tied together only

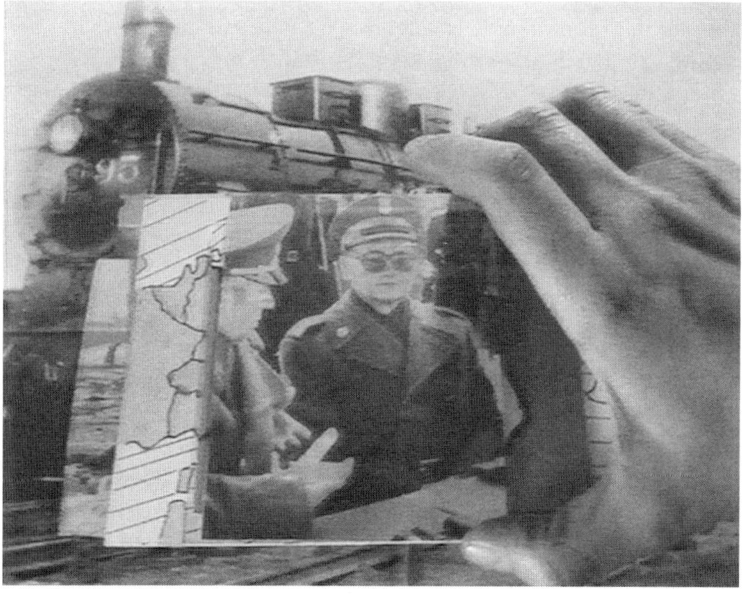

Figure 4. Train pedagogy. © Films du Fleuve |

because they have come into contact with this knot of lies. In the face of propaganda, the film insists on other uses of language. One interviewee speaks of how bad grades in Russian classes were interpreted by the authorities as political resistance, whereas the study of Polish literature was encouraged by the Church. The film ends on an elegant piece of "parole errante" in the form of a poem lamenting the loss of a public sphere: it ends with the verse "Only Poland has a tomb."

Flashes of Hope

The Dardennes' last and most polished documentary, *Regarde Jonathan*, returns to the relation between history and its effects, this time through an exploration of the life and work of the playwright Jean Louvet, considered "the most important theater writer in Francophone Belgium in the last quarter of the 20th century" (Dubois 2006, 349). The son of a miner, Louvet rose through the educational system to become a professor. But around the time of the general strike, he decided to alter his career path and founded the Proletarian Theater in a gymnasium in the working class town of La Louvière, where he has remained since. Despite this renewal of his ties to the Walloon working class, Louvet's identification with it is wrought with tension.

The Dardennes multiply the number of stylistic effects to explore this divided identity, interweaving sequences of performances of Louvet's plays, pure fiction, readings performed by Louvet, scenes of life in Wallonia (including shots of the carnival), interviews, and archival footage of the general strike. The opening sequences illustrate how stylistically self-conscious the Dardennes' documentaries can be. The film opens with a long close-up on rippling water accompanied only by lapping on the soundtrack. Slowly the title appears scratched in red over the water. The sound of a barge's engine hums low in the background, becoming ever more defined, until we hear its horn. The camera by now is panning up, showing the barge and the factory-lined banks of the Meuse. It slowly pans to the highway on the other side of the river, as we hear distant police sirens, until the pan ends on a deserted factory yard with flashing streetlights hung from power lines. With a cut to a black screen, the sound fades out and is replaced by the sound of deep breathing. A fade-in brings the viewer into a boxing ring, explaining the sound—it is the solitary boxer's breathing as he bounces around a ring, ducking and counterpunching an imaginary opponent. The image is in overdeveloped grainy black and white (the contours of the boxer's body have become blurry). A voiceover explains that the first performances of the Proletarian Theater, of Louvet's play *The Train of the Good God,* took place in a community boxing ring on evenings on which no fight was scheduled. A blue title appears over the image: "the night speaks to the night." There is then an abrupt cut to a passing train through some rubble on the outskirts of the city. All this technical mediation points to a disconnection between the "train of history" and present life. Archival footage—"images that have prevented seeing" according to the voiceover—is treated ironically, repeated, sped up or slowed down unnaturally, overwritten with ironic text (figure 5).

The Dardennes found in Louvet's plays much of the same thematic interests that they have explored throughout their own career, including the relationship between father and son. Their camera tracks laterally across a set somewhere between a kitchen, a living room, and a factory: a stove, some chairs, a kitchen table are arranged on shipping pallets that double as the floor, spread out in Louvet's gymnasium/theater during his play *Conversations in Wallonia.* This mechanical pan often misses dialogue, sending the voices off screen almost inadvertently. The mother and the father speak of the past, of school, of the father's return from the

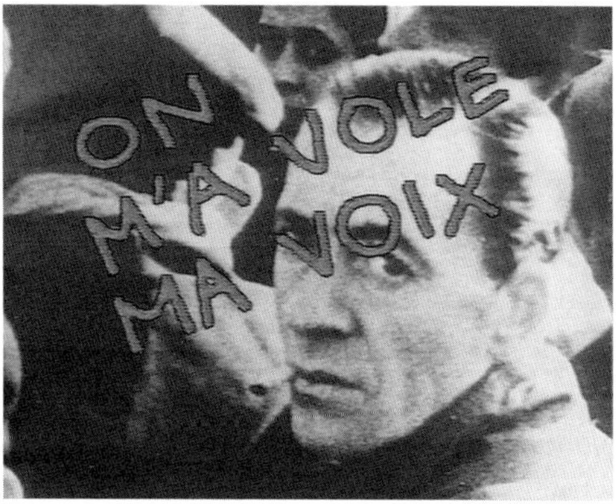

Figure 5. "My voice has been stolen." © Films du Fleuve

war, of his work in the factory, and of the new opportunities opening up through education to the boy, Jonathan. But the dismal steel buttresses, the exposed ductwork of the theater disappoint, as does the stitching together of the archival shots, the lonely boxer, the vague terrain, and the industrial landscapes. The world has changed, but something has faded: the family, the individual's relation to others.

The film includes readings and performances of several other plays, including *l'Homme qui avait le soleil dans sa poche,* about the assassination of the communist leader Julien Lahaut in 1950. Through Lahaut, the film touches upon an important theme of Belgian national history through the "question royale."[1] During the coronation of King Baudouin, someone in the crowd pronounced loudly, "Vive la république!" Lahaut, a deputy in the National Assembly at the time, clearly repeated the phrase for all to hear. A week later he was dead; and in Seraing, 300,000 attended his funeral. Here, however, Lahaut is himself shown as a ruin, in a close pan of the massive statue at his tomb, a close-up of his hand is juxtaposed with a text proclaiming "the sidewalks are empty"—again insisting on the lack of solidarity. A montage sequence combines wasted factory yards with archives of the strike, images of the hammer and sickle, an archival film of Lahaut's mother leading the funeral procession and holding his portrait, images of wintry factory courtyards, leaden frames with traces of broken glass floating in the wind.

Louvet is interviewed alone, appropriately in a moving train car. The moving train of history cannot be stopped, but he can speak from its inside. He describes *Le train du bon dieu* (another train) as a train heading for a better world, again evoking the utopian promises of *Léon M.* and *Le journal.* But Louvet also speaks poignantly of his disappointment with "totalizing ideology"; Marc Quaghebeur has written that Louvet "penetrates the mutilating consequences of a modern era blocked between the reified individualism of the market circuit and the totalitarian second coming promised by the liturgies of mass movements" (Quaghebeur 1984, 15). Louvet is interesting for the Dardennes, for he gives an example of how to proceed as a creative artist when collective identification and mastery of history are not possible. He explains that he now works by physical "flashes"; he has turned his back on "fables of history." He proceeds by moments of "arrachement," or uprooting, when basic human drives, desires, and empathy uproot him from the so-called "processes" of history. He resembles more and more Schmerling's man of Engis, daily confronting the basics of human life—love, reproduction, homemaking, death—constantly readjusting his perception and his physical reactions to an ever-changing environment.

There is one brief scene near the beginning of the film that contains neither dialogue nor montage, and which anticipates some of the Dardennes' later work with camera position and cutting. The camera is set close to a train track, upon which a train is already passing through the visual field. With the unmotivated cut and the proximity of the camera, the train first appears as unidentifiable colors, a blur of yellow and green and a rumbling before the viewer recognizes it as a train, giving the impression that we are catching up to an already unfolding action. Evoking Louvet's title, this train suggests the confusion that takes place when the train of history ineluctably passes by. But the effect is more physical than allegorical: The viewer's eyes are drawn from right to left by the pure movement, until the train has passed totally through the visual field, leaving a fixed view of a wintry industrial *terrain vague*. Again, even with the fixed camera, the effect is disconcerting in that the eyes first must adapt to a pure movement and then readapt to the extreme stasis of history's aftermath. The brothers' camera seems to strike on a less "discursive" way of looking at history, their own brand of "flash," forcing our eyes literally to adjust to its passing.

These documentaries may seem to paint a rather bleak picture of history: Political aspirations come to ruin and the *prise de parole* leads to cacophony. If history is a battle, the films seem to admit defeat. But one can also perceive an important, more optimistic strain in the Dardennes' filmmaking. As in Louvet's writing by flashes or in the images of the Meuse, there is an intermittent plea to utopian desire and hope. It is interesting that the Dardennes had begun preparing at least one other documentary during this period, this one about the philosopher and author of *The Principle of Hope*, Ernst Bloch. According to Douglas Kellner, Bloch believed that "hope permeates everyday consciousness. . . . For Bloch, individuals are unfinished, they are animated by 'dreams of a better life,' and by utopian longings for fulfillment" (Kellner n.d., 1, 2). Luc Dardenne explains his interest in Bloch: "Of Ernst Bloch, I would say that the idea that we retained, in our work, was that utopia for him . . . is something that, in individual or collective acts, produced at a certain moment in History, escapes the historical moment at which the events take place" (Dardenne 1996–97, 33). Hope happens inside the train of history, no matter where it is going. History begins to recede from their *mise-en-scène*, but people, their relations, their desire for fraternity, do not.

Falsch (1987)

It was around this time, however, that a chance viewing of the Dardennes' *Regarde Jonathan* gave them the chance to grow again and bring their concerns one more step toward a larger audience. Their first full-length film came in 1987 with *Falsch*, an adaptation of a play of the same name by a Jewish-Belgian writer named René Kalisky (1983). Although fictional, the film has much in common with their documentaries and appeared only on Belgian television. The brothers first considered working on the play at the suggestion of Marc Quaghebeur, a cultural minister, who had admired their way of filming Louvet's work in *Regarde Jonathan*. They had even originally planned to shoot on video, but they had the opportunity to work with a well-known director of photography named Walter Vanden Ende (who later shot Jaco Van Dormael's worldwide hit *Toto le héros*, 1991) if they agreed to work in 35mm. *Falsch* thus inflated into a feature, but one that remains tied closely enough to the original text that it is rather hybrid, an incremental transition to fiction.

Like the documentaries before it, *Falsch* is concerned with history and memory, or in the words of Jean-Marie Piemme, with "taking from the dead the part of the future that lies within them" (Piemme 1996–97, 9). In this case the dead are the victims of the Shoah. Kalisky, whose father was deported from Belgium in 1944 and died in Auschwitz, wrote at a fertile moment for the discussion of issues suppressed in French and Belgian society: fascism, the occupation years, and the Shoah. In the now famous history of the "Vichy Syndrome" sketched by Henry Rousso (1990), cinema and literature—with works like Marcel Ophuls's *Sorrow and the Pity* (1969) or Patrick Modiano's *Place de l'étoile* (1968)—played a vital role in drawing attention to unhealed wounds of the past, including the effects of anti-Semitism and deportation on Jewish families and individuals. Kalisky began writing plays dealing with such subjects as early as 1972 and continued to do so until his early death in 1981 as he was completing *Falsch*.

Kalisky's play examines the thickness of the Shoah in the memory of the lone survivor of a Jewish family from Berlin. The play is set in a dark and altered space, a disco in 1970s New York from which wafts strains of a synthesized version of Strauss waltzes. Joseph Falsch, a middle-aged doctor who emigrated to the United States from Berlin in 1938, is lured to the disco by this nostalgic music. A provocatively dressed firebrand named Lilli takes his arm in the line that has formed outside the entrance. But a black man named Gus grows angry when Joe passes before him: a fight breaks out and Joe falls, his head hitting the asphalt. When he returns to consciousness, Joe is inside the disco, surrounded by his family, or rather their ghosts, for he is the only member to have survived until this time. The others had either died in the camps or accompanied him to the United States in the thirties and died later. Some of the family members work the music in the disco while others are merely guests from the beyond. Lilli turns out to be Joe's first love from Berlin, whom he left behind on his way to America; Gus is his brother, a blackface vaudeville performer. During the rest of the play, the characters return to the moment of their separation and resume stunted relationships that have simmered for decades. In their arguments, the family members explore their relation to each other, to Germany, the relation between victim and victimizer, and the relation between generations.

Again, as in the documentaries, the bridge between history and the present is a memory-infused technical style. *Falsch* emphasizes a break from Joe's normal life by beginning with a strange space, a deserted airport. (The film was shot over fifteen nights at the Ostend airport.) This space is emphasized in the many full or long shots of lonely individuals in the cavernous emptiness. The action starts out oddly, with a tracking shot of a man, inexplicably in blackface (figure 6) roller-skating through the airport, his movements choreographed to the macabre-sounding Strauss. Another man approaches from the opposite direction; when they meet, they rapidly embrace, while the skater does a swift pirouette and skates off again, two bodies meeting briefly in the night. We then cut outside to an image of the airport from a passing car; beyond a barbed-wire fence surrounding the runways a small plane lands, making a mysterious

Figure 6. A strange *mise-en-scène.*

delivery. A woman (Lilli) looks through the fence as her taxi pulls away. A closer view of the plane shows the propellers coming to a stop and Joseph stumbling out of the plane alone. Inside the airport clumsy, balding men continue their bizarre gyrating. Other family members arrive at this macabre party. Even the scenes of dancing show the couples far apart, performing noticeably different dances, in a space that has no relation to what they are doing. Time and space are presented from the perspective of Joe's inner turmoil, as the various characters turn out to be the unnatural colonization of the present with the ghosts of Joe's memories.

The film does not recount a chronological narrative, but a long and often bitter settling of accounts between family members, all presented equally realistically, through which we gradually deduce a story. Joseph was a promising young scholar in love with Lilli, a beautiful young non-Jewish girl of whom his parents did not approve. The rise of Nazism prompted Joseph to leave love and family and reinvent himself as Joe in New York. In 1938 he left behind his parents and a younger brother, Benjamin the musician, but brought along two others: Gustav, who became "Gus" a vaudeville performer and Hollywood actor, and Georg, who became a renowned painter. Some time after their departure, while

Joe (following in his father's footsteps) was becoming a prestigious doctor, the rest of the family—Jacob the father, his spouse Rachel, the brothers Oscar and Benjamin, the young daughter Bela, and Mina, the mother's sister—were arrested, and eventually died in the camps. The three brothers never recovered from the disappearance of their family. After a career in silent film, Gus was reduced to playing Nazi SS officers in the talkies because of his accent and died a cocaine addict. Georg retreated into an artistic loneliness that ended in his suicide.

Time has been stopped, debilitated by these memories. In one complex scene, the camera scans the onlookers and rests on Lilli before cutting back to Joe, who confesses, "I left because of her." A classic subjective cut opens up a flashback showing a ship in the night, presumably the one that brought Joe to New York. But the voice of Joe's mother intervenes, reminding everyone that the day of his flight was also the day of Ben's first concert as a conductor. Suddenly the camera returns from the ocean liner to the airport, to the tarmac outside, as Joe's desire to remember Lilli is immediately frustrated by the memory of his brother's concert. Even that memory is frozen in a shot depicting Ben standing in the night with a conductor's baton, looking at some kind of glass corridor in the airport, in which there sits a small orchestra. Wafts of Schoenberg reverberate on the soundtrack. But Ben, though enthralled, and the orchestra remain frozen, motionless. Later we learn that Ben was denied entry to the conservatory and that he died in the camps after performing only this one time; at least until now, when he turns the disks of freakish Strauss on the sound system of the airport in Joe's present state. This flashback would like to travel in time but instead it juxtaposes past and present, debilitating them both. Joe laments that he has been wandering on all fours "like a dog among [his] memories."

At the end of Joe's reminiscence, the family members come together on the tarmac, in front of the plane and around the stretcher, for a discomforting family portrait seen in full shot: static, dark, the wind blowing through their hair, and Bela, the youngest sister (the only character invented by the Dardennes), all looking at Joe. Disincarnate voices echo off screen, inhabiting the night that surrounds them: "Why did we stay in Berlin?" "I wouldn't leave my country even though the Nazis wanted me to stop practicing medicine." "Hitler drove Ben out of the academy." Rachel the mother speaks bitterly of her hatred for Joe's father. Ben's concert music slowly gives way to Penderecki's haunting vocal piece *Dies Irae: The Auschwitz Oratorio.* Combined with the soundtrack, this portrait scene represents perhaps the "falsest" of all the incarnations of the Falsch family: The memories of happy childhood that we might expect from looking at a portrait are frustrated by the bickering and the haunting music. The past haunts the present and the stasis of the portrait suggests that there is no future.

Joe's memories ruin his chances at love and family, themes always associated with the future for the Dardennes. Much of the dialogue involves the family's feuds and neuroses, often present in Kalisky's plays: The father is having an affair with his wife's sister Mina; Rachel is overbearing; the family despises Lilli because she isn't Jewish. Other critics have been interested in the ambiguous sexual infantilism in which many of Kalisky's characters are stuck (Silvestri 2006, for example). Joe's distance from his father is combined with a stifling proximity to his mother Rachel, who takes advantage of a waltz to dance extremely close to him, pressing her body against his with a hint of incestuous attraction. Sexually handicapped, Joe's relationship with Lilli is a combination of tenderness and violence: Each encounter begins with a tender glance and embrace but ends with his violently attacking her.

Joseph, Jacob, Benjamin, Rachel—these names and many details of the narrative give *Falsch* an indelible stamp of the Old Testament. Following Kalisky's play, the film contains the Dardennes' first of many rewritings of biblical stories through a contemporary, historical situation. Here Joseph's story seems to represent an impossibility of healing through psychological means. Stephen Frosh has given a suggestive psychoanalytic interpretation of how the biblical Jacob's desire for a peaceful "end of history" is savaged by the attack on Joseph falsely reported by his brothers (Frosh 2005, 185). Through the trouble caused by Joseph's abduction, Jacob becomes aware of another narrative, that of the Covenant, obscure and uncontrollable, in which he is but a part, and which is perhaps revealed only in rupture and dreams. The difficult years that pass by in the Bible, the plagues and suffering, the transformation of Joseph from servant to viceroy, eventually end in a reunion of the family in harmony with God's plan. Like Freud, who evoked the biblical figure of Joseph as a reader of dreams, Joseph attempts to interpret this dreamlike transportation to an airport with his family. He first attempts to refuse the dream, then to engage with it and resolve the conflicts it reveals. But he is no longer a child working through family issues, only a "false" adult in a false family. But if, as Frosh reminds us, Freud considered the use of interpretation of dreams and psychoanalysis as a means of converting "hysterical misery into common unhappiness" (2005, 190), Joe's failed dream interpretation, haunted by the Shoah, does not bring him the calm to carry on.

One begins to wonder what happened to that Dardennian view of history, their attempts to bring out the utopian desire of the past, the "part of the future" that lies in the dead. It is present, but most tenuously. Gazing over the full shot of the Falsch family portrait, one is struck by the handsome faces and by all the different stories to which the Shoah put an end. Often the camera lingers over one face while another character speaks, as the Dardennes attempted to depict a disembodied language, but one that circulated its lost potentialities throughout the film (Dardenne 1996–97, 64). In front of the stretcher during the portrait scene stands Bela, the figure of innocence invented by the Dardennes, whom Joe often takes in his arms, and who is reminiscent of another cinematic child from the same year, Raphaël from *Au revoir les enfants.* Both of these children represent stolen histories, wandering futures whose possibilities haunt the spectator.

As Jean-Pierre somewhat cheerfully remembers, the film did not leave an indelible impression in its wake (Dardenne 2005, 29). In part this is due to the adaptation's enormous debt to the aesthetics of the original. In his theater Kalisky explored what he termed the "surjeu" and the "surtexte": over- or super-acting and over- or super-text. Before the space of the theater and the bodies of the actors there exist a vision and a text that swallow up actors and spaces. In the film, this often leaves the audience feeling rather disconnected, far on the outside looking into Joe's world. The unnatural and empty spaces, the period costumes, the self-conscious camera movements, the avalanche of dialogue, but especially to the use of the actors contribute to this effect. Some of the secondary actors especially, all of whom came from the stage (there was no casting call for the film, only the brothers working from their memories of performers they had seen), seem almost uncomfortable, or at least make the viewer feel rather queasy. This may be a way of teaching the viewer not to assume the subject position of the victim;

but it is legitimate to wonder whether the proscription against losing oneself in the fictional had not worked against the Dardennes' natural empathy. The pane of their window on others was too opaque.

The Dardennes did, however, learn one important lesson about directing actors that helped push them out of a documentary mindset, a lesson that would be more forcefully applied in their later work. Once they had moved into fiction, they realized, perhaps too late for this film, that exploring form was no longer their most important task. With fiction they were dealing with people whom they could and even had to direct through space. They credit their lead actor Bruno Cremer with opening their eyes. Cremer gives a virtuoso performance in a difficult role, playing a sexagenarian with the libido of a twenty-year-old, a strong sick man, a man filled with both love and hate for his family, a man who is here but lost in the past as well. But the lesson was not connected with this virtuosity; it was rather with the way Cremer moved his body: "We began to understand that an actor is a body and a voice that comes out of that body. And a gaze . . . With Cremer, we felt like we were directing a body, from one place to another, who must or must not touch another body, who must take the child in his arms. It was our first discussion of the placement of a child's head on the shoulder of an adult" (Dardenne 2005, 28). The "child's head on the shoulder" is of course that of Bela, picked up in Joe's arms for a few moments during one scene. The act is quickly passed, hardly noticeable. But slowly, once the stylistic mediations are eventually abandoned, acts like this of touching and carrying will move out into the center of their aesthetic. Though *Falsch* starts and finishes with the opacity of history, realizations such as these indicate a move from identity to relation, from psychology to a more hopeful encounter, from expression toward movement and touch.

Against Speed

The short film *Il court il court le monde* (1987) could be seen as the official beginning of the Dardennes' career as fiction filmmakers. *Falsch* was considered a television film or a semidocumentary and was financed to a large extent by the Belgian theater commission. This status explains the existence of *Il court il court le monde;* for at the time, the Commission for the Selection of Films of the French community required the submission of a short work from all filmmakers applying for funding of a feature. The brothers submitted the twelve-minute *Il court il court le monde* so that they could make their next film, *Thinking of You* (1992). Appropriately, the narrative, which recounts a day in the life of a producer of a television program, takes the act of filmmaking as its main subject.

The action begins *in medias res,* with a camera placed in the back of a car watching the driver and passenger in the front seat, played by Jean-Pierre and Luc Dardenne, a rare appearance of the brothers in their films. The car suddenly jolts to a stop as the passenger, Luc, turns around holding a movie camera. We are in the midst of an urgent-sounding argument that takes place in hushed tones. The viewer gradually surmises that they are arguing over the best way to make a tracking shot of the Meuse. Once they agree to drive, a voice says "first drive fast and then slow down." Luc Dardenne's body jerks around in the car as it lurches ahead; he is not in control, but holds onto the camera tightly. As in the shot of the train in *Regarde Jonathan,* the viewer's position is joggled and disoriented, sped up and slowed down. We then see the credits. This sequence is just a prologue to the main body of the film.

A cut brings us to a television studio with a producer, Jean, and editor as they piece together a film devoted to the theme of speed in modern life. We first hear Jean's voice call out, "War is a question of speed!" The phrase is surely inspired by the work of Paul Virilio (1991), author of the *Aesthetics of Disappearance* and theorist of "dromology" (the "science" of speed) and critic of modernity. Virilio has argued that modernity and speed are closely related as a result of the organizing potential of war. He deploys his critique of speed in modern culture through readings of the cinema and television, where images of speed come to replace real life, making the latter disappear. The scene of the Dardennes trying to shoot the site of memory is appropriately and quickly buried under a landslide of images of speed, resulting in a "collapsing of topographical memory" under a supersaturated "utilization of visual prostheses" (Stevart 1996–97, 39). One key element of Virilio's theory is that because its technology evolved from optical research in the domain of war, the cinema lends itself to exhilaration-inducing images of speed and destruction. Jean's film consists of a montage of such images: athletes, cars, atomic explosions, the *Ariane II* space launcher (which had its inaugural run in 1987), clips from classical film and pornographic movies, all interspersed with quotations from Filippo Marinetti, the futurist poet who flirted with fascism, and a key figure for Virilio, and who actually shows up as a character toward the end of the film.

The Dardennes milk these themes to show to the Belgian film community's financial decision makers that they can competently construct a film. But they do so in a sardonic tone, deriding the ideology of speed through a style that is no longer a search for meaning as in the documentaries, but ironic. The *mise-en-abyme* gives an ironic distance to Jean's film: Viewed in the editing studio on a tiny screen, the nuclear explosions lose their force; the sex becomes laughable. Working with their editor Marie-Hélène Dozo for the first time in their long collaboration, the brothers cut back and forth between the *Ariane* launch, nuclear explosion, and sexual climax with the editor's incredulous comments as voiceover. Jean is treated with equal irony, and the editing technique constantly slows down this wannabe mover and shaker. He receives a call from Sophie, a former girlfriend, who is apparently in town from New York. He excitedly drives home to meet her, but in his compact car he couldn't be further from the ideal of Marinetti on his motorcycle; in frustration, he honks away at a slow-moving delivery truck until he is finally rear-ended by another car. (The film ironically cuts to footage of an atomic explosion.)

By the end of the film, the barrage of images devolves into absurdly incoherent representations of time and space. Back in his apartment, shaving, Jean speaks excitedly to himself about New York and adventure until the telephone rings, announcing his girlfriend Sophie's arrival. Here the Dardennes ironically cut the action up into fragments. More than Marinetti's hymns to speed, the film resembles a spoofed version of Buñuel's *Chien Andalou*. The Dardennes first use a silent film intertitle that reads A FEW SECONDS LATER. They then chop the action into a series of static images. We hear the sound of tires screeching to a halt outside, off screen, and we hear Jean calling out for Sophie. The next shot brings us into the street, where we see, lying in the street in front of Sophie's car, an elderly man whom she has just killed. The dead man could be seen as a critique of Jean's aesthetics of disappearance as he glances up toward Jean and recites a bit of *franglais* Shakespeare: "être vu ou ne pas être vu [to be seen or not to be seen], that is the question."

Of course, Jean barely glances at him; he is too much on his way. The film ends on a cutaway of Marinetti picking up Sonya—Jean's assistant and object of his abusiveness on the set—on his motorcycle in the studio: They wear blissful expressions as he revs his engine.

This clever film mocks Jean's quest for speed, both in film and life. But the prologue has difficulty fitting in with the rest of the piece. It seems to express a desire for another type of image, one that respects the integrity of actual spaces and people. The jostling around inside the car (an extremely important setting in the Dardennes' later work) evokes the Dardennes' later attempts to "catch up to the action" (Héliot 2005, 129), rather than an illusion of speed, edited together with the greatest of ease from some of society's most common images. (Jean does not even film himself but weaves his montage from the public store of pornographic and war images.) As Marc-Emmanuel Mélon points out to the brothers themselves, this early fiction period was marked by their desire to locate a different image, a different way to touch the viewer: "that has been your problem since the beginning; how to situate yourselves in relation to existing images, as how to situate yourself in relation to histories already told" (Dardenne 1996–97, 86). *Il court il court le monde* batters us with images, but these are not the Dardennes'. It is interesting to note that, despite all the film's *mise-en-abyme*—the film of Jean making a film, the film Jean makes, the film of the Dardennes making a film—there is one film that is absent, the Dardennian film that Luc shoots from the passenger seat.

Punching the Clock: *Thinking of You* (1992)

The brothers' first full-length picture, *Je pense à vous* (*Thinking of You*), made while they were in their early forties, should have inaugurated a major career. They had a subject they had been preparing since at least 1985 (a film called *Jobless Vulcan* [*Vulcain chômeur*] that had been encouraged by Henri Storck) about the effects of unemployment on a Séresien steel-working family. They had a decent budget that permitted large-scale shooting, well-known actors and professional crew members, even a world-renowned scenarist from the pantheon of the *nouvelle vague*, Jean Gruault. The success of films from Belgium (Dormael's *Toto le héros* and Rémy Belvaux's *C'est arrivé près de chez vous / Man*

Bites Dog, 1992) and the burgeoning independent film industry seem to imply a growing audience for the edgy films on which the Dardennes have since set their imprimatur. They had finally meandered into the center of the city.

And yet, in December 1991, even before *Thinking of You* was screened publicly, Luc Dardenne judged the film bitterly: "What now? Forge ahead in the cinema? Continue making films? What good is that! The bad film we just made should cure us forever of that illusion, of that pretention" (Dardenne 2008, 10). Nor were the brothers alone in their contempt: The film was snubbed by distributors (it appeared briefly on French television in July 1992) and by all the important film journals. Their career seemed over: "after *Je pense à vous*, the world of Belgian cinema was whispering that they had witnessed our suicide" (quoted by Andrews 2006). Time has not changed many minds: *Thinking of You* remains the Dardennes' least favorite and least representative film, and it is rarely mentioned in critical studies of their work.

Despite this glum reaction, the ninety minutes of *Thinking of You* are not completely unendurable. The film sets out from the social and geographical content dear to the brothers: the disappearance of the working class, the crippling of a family by unemployment, the smokestack-dotted landscape of Seraing, and the debt of present generations to the past. It opens where the precredit sequence of *Il court il court le monde* left off—with images of the Meuse from a passing car, this time in a more traditional establishing shot. The camera cuts to a mid shot of the main character, a contentedly smiling Fabrice Ferraro (Robin Renucci) driving with his wife along the Meuse, steel furnaces behind, flowers and a luggage carrier on top of their car. Fabrice, Céline (Fabienne Babe), and their son are moving into a new house, built near the river. In the next sequence, family and friends gather to celebrate their move; in the new garden, Fabrice bashfully embraces his beautiful wife in front of the coworkers, everyone dances together, and the scene ends with a group shot of the family gathered around a cake.

The link between family harmony and work is underscored throughout the film, as when the young daughter of a worker gives a protest speech after the government proposes a new "plan acier" for the steel plants. Much of Fabrice's contentment is anchored in his self-identification with his job in the blast furnaces. Like his father before him, he is looked up to as a leader in the community, playing an important role in the annual Carnival preparations, a longstanding Wallonian tradition, and transmitting this tradition to his son by teaching him the steps of a traditional dance and a trumpet tune. The film's details closely reflect the demographics and traditions of workers in Seraing, down to the family's Italian name and the specially made Polish clogs that Céline's father bequeaths to her son and which link the Ferraros to the many immigrants in Seraing. This family culture is not overidealized, as we see when Fabrice shows his son the cemetery of discarded barrels that dot the grass-covered slag heaps surrounding Seraing. Fabrice explains to his son that whenever a man loses his footing and falls into a vat of molten steel, his coworkers preserve it, bringing it into the woods that have grown up over these mounds of debris. He stops to show his son the "grave" containing his eviscerated grandfather.

After the inevitable layoff, Fabrice begins to slowly abandon family life, becoming a depressed shell of his previous self. The narrative focuses on his jealousy toward Céline, whom he sees as a prize he doesn't deserve. The film introduces side narratives, one including his brother, who has left the factory to open a printing shop (an act representing for Fabrice a rejection of the factory life), and who has always coveted Céline. The other concerns Céline's English instructor—she is learning English to improve her job prospects, perhaps suggesting a changing, globalizing economy—a young man from Manchester named Jack. During one dramatic scene, Fabrice storms out of an awards ceremony at the English school and finally, after months of hiding the truth, tells Céline he has been fired. He forces her to return to Jack, and, even though there is nothing happening between Céline and Jack, a few days later he awkwardly offers her to him as a gift. Fabrice's descent, filmed with gloomy lighting and music, touches all his family relations: He forgets to pick his son up from school, takes him out in the middle of the night, stares despondently at the Meuse, and disappears. Everyone assumes he has jumped in the river, like the many stories of suicide by drowning that the Dardennes remember from childhood. Instead he winds up at *la Sirène*—the Mermaid—a tavern and whorehouse where he drinks himself to sleep night after night, tooting away at a kazoo instead of his trumpet.

Two events take place to eventually bring Fabrice back. First, his brother Laurent, who turns out to be a client of *la Sirène* during business trips, discovers Fabrice and tells Céline where to find him. When she arrives, she speaks only a few words: "We are waiting; we need you." It is a strong scene, and yet her simple plea does not entirely convince Fabrice, as if love and family were not really the issue. The real issue is revealed a few days later, during one of Fabrice's jobs as a day laborer. There he witnesses the beating of a man who, after being summarily fired, had threatened to report the boss. This scene revives Fabrice's passion, and he violently thrashes the supervisor, quits work, and walks with the man through the countryside back toward Liège. As Martin O'Shaughnessy has argued, this scene reflects a subtle understanding of changing economic conditions in the early 1990s (O'Shaughnessy 2005). If trade unions and family provided solidarity in Fabrice's recent past, it must now be found elsewhere, in the recognition that suffering did not end with the closing of the factories, that in fact it pops up in less-organized and protected forms. Fabrice's return to life is brought about by his family, but even more by a moment of empathy and solidarity with a stranger, in a hint of the Levinas-inspired ethical encounters that are central to later films.

When Fabrice arrives in Seraing, the Carnival festivities are in full swing, and, as in *Regarde Jonathan*, the film revels in images of the parades. Fabrice is first shown in shot-countershot arrangement observing the merry procession, the musicians, the rhythmic foot stomping, the traditional tossing of oranges. A point-of-view shot falls on Céline, elegantly dressed and watching their son, who dances as his father had taught him. Suddenly the boy's eyes fall on his father and he runs from his mother's side. Céline glances across the parade toward the camera. The boy pitches an orange to his father, who lobs it across the parade to Céline, and the next shot shows the family reuniting. Finally, one of the marchers hands Fabrice a trumpet, and as he begins to play, the camera pulls back in a striking crane shot, rising above the family, as they become engulfed in the crowd. Fabrice has returned to the harmonious fabric of the family, the city, and the history of Seraing.

So why did the Dardennes consider *Thinking of You* so embarrassingly mediocre? The problem was not in communication—they had the means to reach a broad audience. Instead, the problem lies in the process of filming, one that led to a product lacking in affective intensity.

The brothers have expressed two basic but related discontents with documentary filmmaking. The first was the understandably reserved attitude that many subjects of their documentaries took to their prying questions and imposing camera. In documentary they "felt a limit, a resistance coming from those we were filming and from the way in which events were unfolding" (L. Dardenne 2008, 110). There had also always been a problem of access to the historical event in the documentary, as if the camera, forced to come after the event, could only film indirect *témoignages*, or the effects of history on individual identities. In a sense, by moving out of documentary, they were hoping to step outside and stop observing others through the window, as they had since they were children. The documentaries are inspired by a desire for encounters, but they often seemed to be defining their subjects from the outside.

Fiction, they hoped, would allow a more intense and reciprocal interaction with crew and actors, of the type they experienced in the theater with Gatti. With Gatti, "we lived as a community and every evening ate together," says Luc. Jean-Pierre adds that "it was with Gatti that things crystallized. Before that everything was in flux, I never belonged to a group" (quoted by Begon 1996–97, 74). The shift would also allow the Dardennes to represent, with emotional intensity, history in the present. As they tell it, "There was the pleasure, the desire rather, to work with actors. To have fun, tell our own stories. And to work on the present. We wanted to take people alone as they are and try to see how, alone, they discover a human language, a manner of being two, of shaking hands, of helping each other" (Dardenne 2005, 25). The collaborative method, it was hoped, would let them tell stories from the inside of history, with the help of creative people who could develop new types of shots and montage; in short, it would create a style born of fraternity.

They evidently had not foreseen the pressures of making a film with professional crews and actors. Conceiving *Thinking of You* began well enough "laughing, drinking and raising hell" with a great screenwriter, Jean Gruault, who had worked extensively with Truffaut and Godard and on Alain Resnais's *Mon oncle d'Amérique* (L. Dardenne 2008, 17). Gruault is a subtle and complex writer whose scripts display thematic commonalities with the Dardennes, and they credit him for showing them how to "extract characters from the clay of documentary" (*Contre Bande* 2005, 33).[2] But the lesson did not serve their own ends, for they also admit to "having been afraid of [Gruault]" (*Desimages* 2005, n.p.).

Without a clear idea of what they themselves wanted to achieve—"we didn't understand what we wanted and we had made ourselves believe that we did"—the collaboration became rather one-sided (L. Dardenne 2008, 17). The result was a literate but involved plot filled with subplots, all atypical of their terse and laconic later work. Like *Falsch* and the documentaries, the film is filled with words.

It was during the shoot that the Dardennes encountered the greatest problems. Years later, they told Geoff Andrews that the film was made "not against us, but without us" (Andrews 2006). The production came with a team of professional crew members and actors, a director of photography, and an assistant director, none of whom was chosen by the Dardennes. Seeing the brothers' hesitations, the crew began to make more and more important decisions for them: Jean-Pierre called them "jackals": "They think that it's for your own good and they take away your film" (Dardenne 2005, 31). Much of the *mise-en-scène,* camera position, and lighting were decided by crew members or even the actors. The first assistant director was replaced before the brothers could obtain a video monitor (a tool they consider essential), but the cameraman had already taken over. They had been frozen out.

The onscreen result is a compendium of conventional effects that fall far short of the images that the Dardennes were looking for. The film is also filled with stylistic "noise." This is evident in the completely clichéd opening sequence, with its establishing shot, zoomed in to the main character, replete with the appropriate details that tell us all we need to know. Later, in melodramatic scenes of Fabrice and Céline arguing, for example, the editing provides a conventional shot-countershot arrangement, with appropriately moody lighting. The extreme overhead long shot at the end is nifty, but mainly because it cost a lot of money, and for its effect of showing the reconciliation of Fabrice and the community borders cliché. These images are reinforced with befitting musical frames. The light Mozart at the beginning of the film reflects the family's happiness, as if we weren't already aware of it from the close-up on Fabrice's face. In more poignant moments we hear the contemporary minimalist Wim Mertens's pensive synthesizer. The diegetic music also tilts toward psychology when Fabrice plays himself a depressed trumpet version of "Happy Birthday," alone in the dark; his kazoo in the whorehouse pounds the audience over the head with his abjection. Accessories are also conventional. Fabrice's suit is simple and respectable like him, but he could easily trade it for his neighbor's; and when he wallows, his clothing becomes appropriately ruffled and dirty. Céline's sexy red dress stirs up his jealousy. The trumpet, the clogs, the house, the oranges, the whorehouse, and all the rest are mere props and symbols rather than objects with their own history or weight. Years later these scenes irk the Dardennes: "we ended up feeling that we were composing images. We try to avoid that at all costs: the sense that everything becomes readable and you can say, 'Oh yes, this element refers to that, there's this diagonal . . .' Do that and you end up losing the fluidity, the energy, the tension" (Romney 2006).

Most disappointing for the brothers may be the use of actors. Fabienne Babe was a much-demanded actress who appeared in several issues of *Cahiers du cinéma* in 1992, gracing the cover in November. Her portrait mentions several directors, names such as Rohmer and Dardenne favorite Ken Loach, but no Dardennes (Strauss 1992, 7). Likewise, the reputation of the male lead, Robin Renucci, having worked most recognizably with Claude Chabrol in *Masques,* dwarfed that of the brothers. Renucci and Babe do a commendable job inhabiting their characters, conveying their anger, depression, and confusion. But all this finally becomes cliché, and categorizing *Thinking of You* as a genre, or a "socially conscious romantic film" as does Mosley, is not far off the mark (Mosley 2001, 192). Indeed, other than the very perspicacious, such as O'Shaughnessy (2005, 2008), most viewers have simply missed the subtle political-ethical dimension and concentrated on the psychological drama of the film.

One can return to screening of films like Bresson's *Un Condamné à mort s'est échappé* and *Au hasard Balthazar* in the Seraing high school to see how frustrated the Dardennes must have felt working with professionals, and how important it was for them to abandon this system. In his *Notes sur le cinématographe,* Bresson's critique of professional acting starts with the observation that the same actor cannot convincingly be Attila the Hun, Mahomet, a bank employee, and a woodsman in different films (Bresson 1975, 25–26). When one actor plays all these roles, he will naturally tend to collapse them into their similarities, asserting an absurd identity between the bank employee and Attila. To make the connection, the professional actor must pass through conventions of gesture, expression, looking, and *mise-en-scène*. The problem is made more acute when the actor portrays characters as systematically caricatured as the disappearing working class of the late 1980s and early 1990s. Ken Loach has lamented that the practices of professional actors have become so ingrained that they rarely represent working-class people without distortion: "There's actually a lot of working-class drama, but you often sense . . . that the people in them are being patronized, although perhaps not intentionally" (Fuller 1998, 17). The touching but risk-free performances bring the film away from the immediate experience the Dardennes were hoping for when moving into fiction. Emotion is not passed on to the viewer, and won't be until the brothers reinvent the actor in their next film.

With *Thinking of You* ends one phase of the Dardennes' career. They had succeeded in bringing their social concerns to the center, but at the cost of producing an insipid film. Money was spent; careers endured; (a few) people spent a couple of hours in front of the television. In an interview about their following film, *La promesse* (1996), the Dardennes compare *Thinking of You* with the factory itself: "we'd noticed that on the previous film, which was not a heavy film, we had felt like the shop floor manager in a factory, which is still a respectable job, but not what we wanted to do" (Andrews 2006). They had not produced a great collaborative film but created employment—at the expense of the unemployed—in which no one is thinking of anyone or anything but getting the job done. The film stuck in the craw of the brothers for years after as a negative lesson against which they would redefine their entire approach.

Behind Our Images: A New Beginning

The next stage of the Dardennes' career begins with a soul-searching self-critique that almost drove them away from making films. Their questions become fundamental: What to do? Change careers? Try again? Much of the reflection after their failure is recorded in Luc Dardenne's artistic diary, first published in 2005 as *Au dos de nos images* (L. Dardenne 2008—literally, "On the Back of Our Images" or "Behind Our Images"), whose first entries date from the aftermath of *Thinking of You*. It is not clear when Dardenne actually began keeping track of his thoughts in this diary or how much it was revised before publication. Its early pages describe an increasing sense of confidence as the brothers develop a clearer sense of what they want from filmmaking. It then becomes a beautiful piece of writing, relating encounters of the day, brief spurts of poetry, thoughts on news events, reflections on literature, philosophy, and other filmmakers, and it is a warehouse of ideas for films they could make.

Groping for a new way of making films, Dardenne begins by exploring his relationship to his brother. The first person plural of the book's title, strange for such an intimate literary genre, refers to the collaboration of the brothers, the "two-headed filmmaker" as they often call themselves. Early in the book Dardenne imagines an autobiographical film that would express the kind of complicity that the brothers shared. It opens in a bedroom, two twin beds, with two boys in their pajamas, a light switch between them. As the room becomes visible, one boy turns the lights off. The other flips them on again; the other off. A voiceover tells the viewer that the nightly dispute over the lights once became so intense that the lights went on and off twenty-four times a second. The game is interrupted when the father enters the room and screams: "turn out the light!" But only for a moment, for when he leaves they go at it again. Finally the father cries out "Silence!" from the hallway. After a moment of complete calm, one of the boys' voices says "camera," the second "action," and the film begins. The parable implies a lack of authorial center in a creative but not always harmonious dialogue between the brothers.

The film of the boys in their bedroom, titled *Pater Noster,* is interrupted by the voice of the father; but the real despot in these pages is the film industry. The first word of *Au dos de nos images* is "resist." Dardenne spews contempt for the kind of films produced in mainstream cinema, with their "putting into images and music an increasingly trivial, flatly obvious, dramatic mechanism" through a limited number of commonly agreed upon "codes" (L. Dardenne 2008, 15). These codes are imposed by financial interests without the slightest concern for engaging or challenging viewers. Artists are reduced to "conceptionist-managers" whose only goal is to keep the "consumer in a state of alertness" (15). Dardenne tells of his frustration watching people walking in and out of an unnamed Columbia Pictures film to restock on popcorn and soda.

In many ways, the problems that sank *Thinking of You* are reminiscent of those that the *nouvelle vague* derided in the *tradition de qualité,* with its old recipes, its reliance on screenplay and actors, its ignorance of changing aesthetic demands in a young, serious audience, and its conception of the director as a mere illustrator. It was against this tradition that Truffaut and others praised a few "auteurs," filmmakers whose work was "as personal as fingerprints" and who controlled every step of the process, from screenplay to the choice of crew and actors (Baecque and Toubiana 2001, 219). In the interview in which they compare *Thinking of You,* the brothers sound like a young Truffaut: "So we worked on the script, and we told ourselves a few things: that we would not work with well-known actors; we would work in locations chosen only by ourselves; the crew around us would only be friends and people chosen by us; and we would organize every aspect of the shoot ourselves. And most of all, we would have the least possible amount of technology, of technical mediation" (Andrews 2006).

The brothers became *auteurs* in regard to industrial ways of doing things, but without the egocentrism or the refusal to admit to the collective process necessary for making a film that sometimes plagues auteurist theorists. Instead, they made this process as collaborative as it had been when they were working and living with Gatti in the theater. They would now work only with a close-knit group of enthusiastic collaborators with an autodidactic mentality: "to have our crew, find actors who really want to work with us, who don't block us with their professionalism, unknowns who won't steer us without our knowledge toward what is already familiar" (L. Dardenne 2008, 14). Relations on the set, from the directors to the assistant directors to the actors and the camera operators would not be restrained by professional distance but would be organized around a fraternal "vibration" (17) as individuals worked together on a shared project rather than toward self-oriented goals. Nowhere is the cooperative mentality more evident than in the Dardennes' work with actors. The brothers now do their own casting, among nonprofessionals or stage actors, choosing unknowns with whom they could sympathize such as Jean-Pierre Duret (on sound), Alain Marcoën (photography), or Marie-Hélène Dozo (editing).[3] With fourteen-year-old Jérémie Renier and with Olivier Gourmet they found just such people. With Gourmet, the brothers speak of "abandoning themselves to each other" (Dardenne 2008). Auteurism becomes ethical.

Against *Thinking of You,* the brothers would also relearn *mise-en-scène* and framing. Film images had become too finely painted, too oriented toward the audience's visual enjoyment, too often "stuffed to the point of bursting but never actually cracking" (L. Dardenne 2008, 9). If *Thinking of You* was made up of clear but flaccid images, they would now turn to a primitive cinematic state that would capture the energy of the set in new images. The brothers wanted to let the actors and the spaces guide their camera. A "cinema without style" would create images of "the rough, brute, unpredictable, and tense state of present reality" (L. Dardenne 2008, 11). The primary goal of the film, borrowing a distinction from the documentary filmmaker Johan Van der Keuken, is to create a state for the viewer rather than a well-crafted image or a language, to bring the viewer to an encounter with this energy. The goal has shifted perceptibly here: instead of telling us how people feel or giving them voice, the film is meant first and foremost to engage our emotion.

These stirrings took four years to result in a film. The delay was caused in part by the slow elaboration of a new screenplay, which took several drafts and long discussions between the brothers. But it was also a direct result of their independence from the funding mechanisms of the industry, and on this point they preferred to endure setbacks rather than accept compromises. It was in 1994 that the brothers founded Les Films du fleuve, to finance *La promesse* but also to support quality films by other filmmakers and in order to generate more income to fund their own projects. (Dérives continues today as a documentary production company.) Finding investors went slowly. In August 1994 they learned that the Centre du Cinéma at de l'Audiovisuel de la Communauté Française de Belgique, to which they had applied for funding, would not be able to meet their request to shoot that winter, costing them a year. A week later the producer Jean-Luc Ormières, who had been involved in *Thinking of You* and had worked with Chantal Akermann and financed Stijn Coninx's film *Daens* (1993), expressed hesitation over a "two-headed *mise-en-scène,*" and the project was delayed again. Finally, late in 1995, the brothers were able to start shooting, and the shifts in their aesthetic sensibility could finally manifest themselves in

La promesse. They felt once again as if they were working on their first film, this time one in which politics, process, and image would make a coherent whole.

La Promesse

Like other films of the mid-nineties, *La promesse* reflects a greater awareness of the politics of globalization: in this case the exploitation of undocumented immigrants from Africa, Asia, and Eastern Europe. The subject inspired a number of filmmakers, who turned their attention to the experience of immigrants and their children in present-day France. Malik Chibane (*Hexagone* [1994], *Douce France* [1995]), Karim Dridi (*Bye Bye* [1995]), Thomas Gilou (*Raï* [1995]), and most provocatively, Mathieu Kassovitz (*La Haine* [1995]), share many common themes and localities and have come to form the *cinéma de banlieue*, one of the most important generic developments of the decade according to Phil Powrie (1999, 14). One major goal of the artists who invented the genre was to bring visibility to groups within France that had been culturally and politically marginalized just as they had been geographically marginalized into the enormous *cités*, or public housing projects, on the outskirts of major municipalities (Tarr 1999, 173). *La promesse* shares with these films an interest in crime, the relations between Europeans and immigrants, race and racism, unemployment, and other themes.

Though the film is still set in Seraing, it contains few references to the national context and has moved completely into the realm of globalization, whose forces are postnational, often working through multinational companies, trade organizations, and individual initiatives as much as governments. Such invisible networks are, in Hardt and Negri's (2001) famous expression from *Empire*, "deterritorialized." The national provenance of the immigrants in *La promesse* provides a clue. Hamidou, his wife Assita, and their son Tiga come—shipped inside automobiles on the back of a transport truck—from Burkina Faso, a former colonial holding of France, not Belgium. Their presence certainly serves as a reminder of the Belgian exploitation of the Congo, but, unlike some *banlieue* cinema, it is not circumscribed within national identities and can only be explained through Empire's newer, more fluid avatars. When asked by a journalist if he "feels Belgian, Wallonian, bruxellois, or European,"

Luc Dardenne can answer only: "I just feel sick when I have to answer that kind of question" (L. Dardenne 2008, 76).

In another change from the documentaries and first fictions, *La promesse* is a film entirely about the present. It depicts only the slightest geographical remnants of a historical past—for example, a rare long shot showing the blast furnace of Seraing in a background—but spaces are disconnected, and the action takes place as if the characters were unaware of them. A postapocalyptic atmosphere pervades the town and the halfway house, which is constantly undergoing repair, its gutters stinking of human waste and the gas heaters breaking down. The omnipresent rubble and burning debris make it difficult to distinguish construction from destruction. The atmosphere echoes some of the early documentaries and Rossellini's *Germany Year Zero* (1948), which the Dardennes have called a model. In the place of a young blond Edmund Moeschke deprived of youth wandering through the rubble of Berlin after the war, we have another boy, Jérémie Renier, strikingly similar, riding his moped through the streets of Seraing. But the film does not emphasize these spaces as their documentaries had, for example in the long shots of Edmund surrounded by walls or the pans of the river.

Certain forces of the present are also hidden, relegated to a menace off screen that manipulates the characters as if they were marionettes. Many viewers have rightly pointed out that the engines of clandestine immigration are conspicuously unseen in *La promesse.* The only visible manifestation is Roger (Olivier Gourmet), a landlord and contractor who transports undocumented immigrants to and from Seraing. Roger maintains a smooth operation, doctoring passports, extorting extra rent for heat, forcing some of the immigrants to repair the house while shipping others off to France, England, or America. Lurking behind him is a colossal system, comprising individuals, governments, and corporations, including a shipping company and a prostitution ring. We hear one side of a telephone conversation from someone who organizes a roundup of *sans-papiers* to placate the mayor; we are never shown the faces of those who deliver the immigrants. Roger's position is ambiguous, since he must be present but would like to escape notice. His nervous movements, loud clothing, and thick glasses effectively hide his face: he avoids eye contact and is in continual motion. He is assisted by Nabil (Hachemi Haddad), who skulks in dark corners spying on the inhabitants.

Leaving so much off screen, the brothers avoid an analysis of the situation so as to observe it, as it were, from inside the experience of the characters. As in many Dardenne films, the narrative explores the theme of paternity. In his journal and in an interview with the Hardt and Negri spin-off journal *Multitudes*, Luc approaches paternity through the myth of Cronos, the Titan who killed his father Uranus and, fearful of an oracle that declared he would be overthrown by his progeny, devoured each of his children at birth. The myth implies so strong an attachment to power that Cronos wants to control time, prevent the present from evolving into a future without his mastery. "The idea when we made *La Promesse* was that today we lived in the time of Cronos who eats his children, who fears dying, who fears losing his life in leaving life to others, and who therefore hastens to kill to conserve his life. We thought that Roger had something of this character that killed his son. Igor is killed by his father" (L. Dardenne 2003).

Roger does not conjure up the image of Cronos devouring his son in the literal and nightmarish way of Francisco Goya's famous painting, but he does "prevent him from living." He forges with his son a number of bonds by which he ensures cooperation: He makes him call him by his first name, makes him participate in the family business, arranges for him to lose his virginity, and even inscribes their false intimacy on his skin with a tattoo and a tight-fitting ring to match Roger's own. A counterpoint to Roger is the gruff but likable mechanic at whose garage Igor is supposed to be following an apprenticeship. He teaches Igor skills and tries to transmit some values—the importance of work and being on time, even education (when he sees Igor's tattoo, drawn by his father, he asks why he doesn't write on paper—"it's not just for wiping your ass you know"). But Roger disrupts Igor's work; whenever we hear the phone ring or an insistent honking we know it is Roger off screen needing Igor to help him with the business. Roger controls, inscribes, amuses, and constrains Igor's very body.

The Dardennes have often described the worker as "a member of a species on its way to extinction" (L. Dardenne 2008, 16). Only once does the film supply a motivation for Roger's participation in this inhuman system, when he counts out some cash he has hidden in the wall and declares to Igor that the house will soon belong to them. Roger's actions are tied to a kind of cutthroat satisfaction of basic needs for himself and his son.

After all, he is also a victim, like Léon M. or Edmund twenty years after the factory closings. But victims often unhesitatingly make more victims, and Roger's view of others is vitiated by a moral fault. He is caught up in the blind pursuit of a dwelling and a place in the economy—or in Levinas's language the "primordial occupying of a site" (Levinas 1969, 37)—and others are mere instruments. To control time means selective blindness, to discard anything that does not fit directly into this project.

As a counterbalance, the Dardennes' camera moves closer and closer to the individual bodies on which globalization works, in order to "re-territorialize" them. The film plays out in a succession of observations of bodies and the ways in which other characters view them. After Igor and Roger, the next important body to come into contact with this system belongs to Hamidou; and it is indeed already marked by the global economy before coming to Europe, as we learn later when Assita mentions that he has lost three toes in a Burkinabe marble quarry. Hamidou sets the crisis of the film in motion when he becomes a cadaver, a body in the most physical sense. One day immigration officers pay a surprise visit to the building site while Hamidou works on a scaffold, in plain sight on an exterior wall. Igor races to tell him to hide, but when Hamidou reaches to turn off his radio, he loses his balance and falls. The boy rushes to his side and ties his belt around his severely injured leg, cutting off the bleeding. But Hamidou senses that he may die and pleads with Igor to take care of his wife and child if he does. Igor then gives the film its title when he promises Hamidou to do so. When the officers leave, Roger returns to the courtyard and discovers the accident. Instead of taking the hurt man to the hospital, he removes the belt, in effect murdering him. That night he and Igor bury Hamidou deep in cement in the courtyard, hoping to eliminate the evidence, just as Igor buries the wallet of an old lady from whom he has stolen it in another courtyard.

La promesse represents Hamidou's death without some of the grisly effects of contemporary film. The film bears a faint resemblance to neo-noir films like the Coen brothers' *Fargo,* in which one botched crime leads to another, engulfing fairly normal characters in an escalation of violence. But Hamidou's murder is treated with discretion, off screen. Igor runs up the stairs to warn Hamidou that the inspectors have arrived and tells him to turn off the radio. The film cuts to the stairwell, as Igor descends we hear a sudden crash outside. Likewise Hamidou is kept from our view once Roger strips away Igor's belt from his leg. Such discretion is a critique directed at artists and the media in general. Luc recounts his recollection of a story about a photographic experiment run in a Nazi camp, in which people in the grip of death were recorded on film. The brothers often disapprove of what they call an aesthetic of the suffering body and complain that there will always be some unscrupulous artist to accept such macabre experiments as a challenge (L. Dardenne 2008, 19, 36). The Dardennes show us a dark side, but they do not relish spilled blood. Though they are interested in some of the most difficult human circumstances, they treat their characters with a lack of morbid cynicism, which remains a staple of their work.

Instead death is shown essentially in its effects on others. The *mise-en-scène* instead emphasizes the physical and moral encounter between Igor and Hamidou (figure 7). As Igor (and the viewer) hears Hamidou tumble down the ladder, he runs back up the stairs to find out what happened. He then descends again and a cut brings us outside to the courtyard in a close-up of Igor's bust, his hands on the splayed Hamidou's shoulders, begging him not to die. The brothers' long-time sound direc-

Figure 7. Filming Hamidou's death.
© Christine Plenus

tor, Jean-Pierre Duret, has placed the microphone close enough so that we can hear Hamidou's breath. Another cut, unmotivated by the action, places our view ten to fifteen feet away from the two, emphasizing the relation between them as opposed to our own contact with the action. Across this cut, we remain with the closely recorded voices. We feel like participants, or close witnesses in the scene, yet at the same time observers of their face-to-face. Their encounter links their bodies but also links Igor to Hamidou morally through his spontaneous promise. After the scene, Igor's body has changed, become confused and unsure; he cannot seem to adequately wash the blood off his legs in the shower and forgets to take his socks off.

Igor's encounter with the dying Hamidou in that courtyard is a critical moment, whose implications are perhaps temporarily unperceived by Igor. He has been forced to confront Hamidou at his moment of death, and he has engaged with him through a covenant. His promise ties his life to Hamidou's and to Assita and Tiga's lives. His experience of time is no longer his own, but ruled by the promise he has made. Like Hamidou, Assita is constantly threatened with erasure, not only because Roger wants to sell her into prostitution, but also in the eyes of societal institutions. Her family has been torn apart, but she cannot get the truth from Roger, justice from the police, or even health care for her son when he falls sick. If globalization functions smoothly by transporting human bodies across national borders, national institutions exploit her undocumented status to ignore her presence.

Igor, however, changes in his manner of looking at Assita. When Assita arrives at the house, he hides in a storage room next to her room and peers at her undressed body through a peephole. This initial gaze might be interpreted as a fetishistic imagining of difference as erotically charged. Laura U. Marks, whose book on transcultural cinema and embodiment, *The Skin of Film,* inflects my interpretation, describes Western fetishism as a strategy of self-distancing from other peoples depicted as mired in temptations of the flesh: "the desire that the bourgeoisie had forbidden itself became embodied in primitivist fantasies" (Marks 2000, 87). But Igor's gaze meets with obstacles and distractions. He first has difficulty catching a clear glimpse of Assita's body through the hole, which is covered by a layer of fabric that obscures our view (figure 8). The subjective shot then is drawn to other objects in the room that

Figure 8. Igor watching Assita. |

become problematic or distracting in some way: a suitcase whose lid she has inexplicably removed, a religious statuette sitting on the table, a shot of Assita sprinkling water from a Perrier bottle around the room. Instead of a voyeuristic gratification, Igor meets a provisional mishmash of found or altered objects that attest to the culture of *bricolage* by which transnational individuals forge new cultures (Marks 2000, 88–89). The suitcase becomes a new bed for her son in an eloquent example of displacement becoming home. She also wears an African robe covered by a thick wool sweater and coat, keeps a sheep and a chicken in the urban wasteland, and transforms a strand of rope into a shoelace.

Igor gradually assumes the responsibility of his promise, as distance gives way to a deeper caring. In order to provide Assita with money, he must sell his father's ring, and he even has it cut off his finger. He crosses the threshold, forbidden by Roger, to her room in order to help her. Eventually he flees the house with Assita to foil his father's plan to sell her; he holes up in the garage of his apprenticeship—the mechanic is out of town—with Assita and Tiga. Through Assita, Igor is drawn to new acquaintances, such as an African woman who helps him pay Tiga's bill at the hospital and who generously loans Assita her passport to make a trip to Carrara, Italy—site of a marble mine like the one at which Hamidou worked in Burkina Faso—where she has some family.

Although Igor comes closer to Assita, his attitude lacks something important through most of the film. Assita talks; she constantly poses questions about her husband's whereabouts, and threatens to go to the police if Igor doesn't help her. But Igor takes minimal steps toward meeting her demands, trying to help, but his bond with his father prevents him from assuming his place in the conversation. In Levinasian terms, his help is incomplete (see Levinas 1969, 72–81, on the importance of discourse to ethics). For Levinas, the face of the other expresses that other's unbridgeable uniqueness and difference, but a distance that can be overcome only through a mutually respectful relationship that depends on language, in the form of conversation and accountability.[4] Ethics involves a link of separate individuals through language. It is precisely this type of speaking that Igor has been lacking. Throughout most of *La promesse,* the Dardennes present language, a reflection of Roger's totalitarian view of the world, with an almost sarcastic skepticism. Igor's first words compose a cynical lie to an old woman from whom he has just stolen. He continues lying in the van, transporting immigrants to the house, this time in the bastardized Franglais of the global economy: "La Meuse, big usine, beaucoup money." Igor simply has no habitual use of words to answer truthfully.

The promise to Hamidou initiates a new type of communication as a response to others that takes some time for Igor to fully acquire. It is only at the end of the film, when his father discovers him hiding out with Assita in the mechanic's garage, that Igor finally decides to break his silence and quit his lies. This encounter takes place as Igor begins to repair Assita's statuette with a drill press. When his father interrupts, Igor attempts to convince him to confess the truth about Hamidou's death: "Let's go, we have to tell her the truth." Roger's only response is a heavy dash across the screen to tackle his son. At this moment, Igor makes a clean break. When Assita hits Roger over the head with a pipe, the bond between her and Igor has progressed to a solidarity, still wordless. Igor chains his father to a block and tackle and gathers Assita's things. After regaining consciousness, Roger hops gingerly on his unchained foot, reaching out for his son. He starts flailing as he manages only to slap himself with the chain, knocking off his glasses. Roger has been unmasked; his face becomes naked, his violence totally visible. He abuses his paternal authority: "Untie me, you are my son." Confronting the naked face of his father Igor spits out his reaction: "ta gueule, ta gueule, ta gueule! [Shut up ! Shut up! Shut up!]," in words that are pure revolt.

Language plays a very different role in *La promesse* from what it had previously for the Dardennes. Gone are the searching voiceovers, long monologues, ghostly voices, and wordy expressions of inner feelings. Words no longer wander; they become rarer and infused with an ethical sobriety. At the very end of the film Igor finally gives Assita a full account of Hamidou's death and burial. The scene takes place in the stairwell of a station, as Igor helps Assita and Tiga board the train to Carrara. He is no longer hedging: he could easily put her on the train and start his life over. Instead, while mounting the stairs to the ramp, Igor lets Assita gain a step and blurts out: "Hamidou is dead." When Assita turns around, he recounts, in remarkably laconic terms that echo Levinas's demand for sincerity and sobriety in the relation with the other, Hamidou's death, his father's desire to avoid trouble, his own obedience ("j'ai obéi"), and exactly where Hamidou is buried. Sarah Cooper has convincingly described this face-to-face in explicitly Levinasian terms (Cooper 2007, 71).[5] Indeed, the film owes, according to Luc, much to Levinas's description of the face as "a first discourse," leading to a more entwined conversation (quoted by L. Dardenne 2008, 53).[6] Igor first addresses Assita's back, but as she turns around he is able to endure her direct gaze for the first time in the film.

Whether Assita will accept Igor's offer of help is not a given: The film ends with Assita returning down the stairs and walking through the tunnel back to the station. *La promesse* ends in a dramatically different register from that of the Dardennes' previous films, a change at the heart of all their subsequent work. Unlike in *Thinking of You,* there is no self-satisfied and clichéd regrouping into a nostalgic class identification. And yet the film also avoids the sense of complete ruin and irrevocable solitude of the early documentaries. The brothers seem to accept the loss of a historic struggle without cynicism or nihilism. Igor has accepted his responsibility, and after a slight hesitation, runs down the station corridor after Assita and Tiga. The dreams of the past may be over, but the film gives the characters at least the hope for a future and the words to bring them there.

A Sensuous Realism

The greatest stylistic difference between *La promesse* and the fictional works that preceded it is the film's impressive power to elicit an audience's empathy and belief, as if the film were taking place in our own world. Reactions like this one, from Mike D'Angelo, are common enough to form a pattern:

> on the second go-round, I experienced *La Promesse* less as "that movie I saw last autumn" than as "that thing that happened to some folks I knew last year." This sensation was so disorienting . . . that I fought against it, by attempting to envision the world beyond the frame as a set—imagining, for instance, the boom operator standing a few feet to Igor or Roger's left, holding the microphone just above their heads, wondering how much longer it would be before somebody called lunch, trying hard not to cough. It didn't work. The illusion was too strong, the verisimilitude too great. (D'Angelo 1997)

Contrary to their method in *Thinking of You,* the brothers will from now on eschew conventions and develop a pure form of realism. One might frame our approach to what I call their "sensuous realism" with a few questions. First, what techniques specifically work to foster a sensuous experience of the fictional world? How does sensuous realism relate to classical, media-based arguments for film realism, many of which make outrageous claims for the indexical capture of reality through film's chemical and optical mechanisms? Finally, how does their new realism bring their viewer into the ethical and political issues (problems of relation, immigration, and globalization) at the heart of the film?

Let's begin by describing the techniques of realism invented, or reinvented by the brothers, to bring the viewer into a direct contact with the objects and bodies of the film. The first step is the loosening of the narrative organization. No longer regarding the screenplay as a preexisting entity to be "illustrated," the Dardennes look forward to seeing the screenplay "burnt in the fire of the film" (L. Dardenne 2008, 25). Comparing the screenplay to the film, one sees, for example, the disappearance of several expository scenes. Such deletions take away the synoptic narrative viewpoint we might usually have, tying us up within the "invisible knot" and the "pure tension" of the situation. Narrative links, like history and the global economy, lurk somewhere off screen.

This loosening is combined with a highly original use of the *plan séquence,* or duration shot, which gives the viewer a greater awareness of time. At times films like *La promesse* hearken back to the tradition of the "integrity of the shot," according to which, as Alan Williams puts it, "a shot, and thus the action or situation it depicts, may be allowed to continue until it attains some kind of formal or narrative closure" (Williams 1992, 126). Elsewhere Williams cites Alexandre Astruc on the relation of shot and action according to this tradition: "So long as the movement has not resolved itself no other image can be tolerated" (30). The integrity tradition thus normally gives a harmony between action and the shot, and the film is felt as a series of temporal units, meshing through a rhythmic editing style rather than one determined by the plot. But the Dardennes' technique aims for intolerability, for action and shot rarely correspond. Their scenes often begin, as Louis Héliot puts it, "as if they were catching up to the action" (2005, 129). Many begin *after* the action has begun and cuts come *before* it has ended, leaving the viewer with an experience of time and movement but little resolution. Cuts are abrupt, sometimes brutal, taking us out of one action and plunging us *in medias res* into another, during which another *plan séquence* gives us a moment to situate ourselves until we are abruptly moved again. Suddenly we see a flash of color, yellow and blue, a swinging door, the texture of a fabric, a lock of hair; and then the familiarity of these colors and textures will become recognizable as a shirt, we will recognize Roger's rump and Igor's hair, and finally we understand that Roger is beating his son, though we do not learn why until the end of the scene. We cannot control time like Cronos, for it is unleashed on us, and yet we are fascinated prisoners of each segment.

The brothers also begin to seriously experiment with the camera and its positioning, an effort that will be developed from film to film. To do so, they renewed their ties to the director of photography, Alain Marcoën, who had helped them with *Il court il court le monde,* and began to collaborate with camera operator Benoît Dervaux. They rejected unwieldy cameras and tracking equipment for a lighter, though still 35mm, shoulder-held camera. This mobile camera, now a staple of their work, underscores the human presence of the camera operator in the film and has a direct impact on how the brothers direct actors and crew-members. Their long sequence shots require that scenes be rehearsed numerous times until an appropriate rhythm has been found for each segment. One brother works closely with the actors and crew, who must be choreographed into the scene as much as the actors, while the other watches on a video monitor, a leftover practice from their documentary days. From the point of view of the sound engineer or the camera operator, there is no perceptible distinction to be drawn between the set and the actors: Everyone moves together in an elaborate choreography. The frame of the scene is invented by the directors, working with the actors and with the crew. The dance makes the "vibration" of the set, doubtlessly inspired by Gattiesque collaboration. Rather than provide an illustration for a story, the shot that the viewer looks at grows organically out of the group's solutions to problems of positioning and movement. Shots built up in this collective way are, according to Luc, "more alive" than what the brothers originally suggest in their screenplays (L. Dardenne 2008, 175).

The Dardennes' frames emphasize a lack of an external point of view, one that would organize and hierarchize the *mise-en-scène.* Coining the term "corps-caméra" (or "body-camera"), Luc emphasizes the camera as a means of encounter, of *contact:* "The movements of Benoît Dervaux carrying the camera are more subtle, alive, more felt and complex than any movement created with the help of machinery. His bust, frame, legs, and feet are those of a dancer. With Amaury Duquenne (his assistant) who accompanies him and supports his movements, the two form a single body-camera" (L. Dardenne 2008, 175) (figure 9). The "body-camera" suggests a reciprocal relation between the terms, one in which vision is not an independent entity but is reseated in the body, or rather in two bodies involved in a dancelike movement through other bodies. The camera is a point of visual contact with the film world, like a prosthetic visual organ with no central control. It moves the emphasis of the film away from the psychodrama of the characters—whose motivations

Figure 9. Benoît Dervaux, Amaury Duquenne, and cinematographer Alain Marcoën. © Christine Plenus

become more mysterious—and onto the physical contact between the camera, the people recording, and the thing recorded.

The body-camera does not provide information to the viewer—it "seeks to follow, it doesn't wait, it doesn't know" (L. Dardenne 2008, 18). To further destabilize our sense of a detached view, the team often attaches to this camera a lens that keeps foreground and background relatively in focus, creating an almost infinite number of framing effects. The operator often screws his attention to an actor who moves quickly, such as the backs of Roger and Igor's heads as they careen down an alley in Roger's van. The cityscape beyond the windshield is in focus but is blurred by its movements, and the viewer is deprived of visual mastery over space. At other times, the camera detaches itself from an individual character in order to follow the links between characters, as when it sweeps from one face to another. In such scenes the background jumps out at the viewers even distractingly because of the vertiginous distortion with which it is presented. Often the camera seems distracted by these objects, as when it turns away from Igor and his father to follow Assita who inexplicably peels a swallow's nest from an abandoned wall.

Without an overall perspective on a solid space, the smallest objects can attract our attention.

This nonnarrative, limited view of the knot of events makes the Dardennes' camera more sensuous. As viewers we are discouraged from using our sight as a means of contemplation and are invited to consider it as a part of our central nervous system, connected to our more intimate senses of touch, smell, and hearing. The Dardennes often brush the viewer up against a "haptic" cinema, to cite a concept adapted from the art historian Aloïs Reigl by Laura Marks in her elegant theory of cinematic touch. For Reigl, the haptic designates artistic practices that predate techniques such as deep space, chiaroscuro, and perspective, which feed the illusion of distance between viewer and object viewed. If vision is often described as the sense of distance, haptic visuality compels the viewer instead to make connections on the surface plane of the image, on its own skin. In her discussion of self-consciously experimental films and videos, Marks enumerates several techniques that do not apply to *La promesse:* scratched film stock, low-quality resolution, striking use of filters, and more. But the camera does produce several effects that one might call haptic. The blurring of background patterns makes objects like the loud wallpaper on the office wall, the curtain separating the bathroom, the embossed walls of the shower, all stand out, breaking down the foreground/background distinction. Faces themselves are filmed so close that the skin, beards, pimples, rotting teeth, and strands of hair become distinguishable textures. Marks's compelling hypothesis is that cinematographic techniques such as these can bring us so close to the film that our sense of touch is aroused.

Sensuous realism demands a good amount of effort on the part of viewers. Objects and bodies become more important but less coded, and we tend to look at them as we do real objects and bodies, as shapes, textures, weights, smells, and relations we investigate. Marks develops a rich vocabulary for describing our way of "excavating" these "fossils," "fetishes," or "recollection-objects" so that we can arrive at some kind of incomplete understanding of them. In part, this happens through an increase in attention and sensibility. We have seen thousands of eyeglasses and cheap shirts like the ones worn by Roger. And yet the camera focuses on his clothing, making us sensitive to their unique color, texture, and shape, and then inserts it in various contexts—we see his shirt flash as he beats his son, as he sings a song, as he makes his rounds, as he searches for Igor and Assita, and when Igor ties him up at the end of the film. Our sensitivity may lead us to formulate more structured and explicit thoughts: We see that the gaudiness of his shirt and the thickness of his glasses, along with his scraggly beard and continual motion, actually hide as much as they reveal. The Dardennes' film world is filled with such overlooked or discarded objects that the camera-body has made tangible and problematic, open to our excavation: faces, skin, blemishes, ears, pallets, scratched doors, wallpaper, brick, wheelbarrow, statuette, radio, jacket, shirt, glasses, wool coat, sweater, hair, fire, bathroom curtain, train tunnel wall, highway; the list would continue until every object of the film is enumerated.

To appreciate the richness of such fossils, one might wander down a digressive path to excavate the meaning of one very important object in the film: Assita's statuette. Commonly a Westerner's gaze on such objects, like Igor's initial view on the eroticized other, is detached and aesthetically appreciative; it might look interesting on our mantelpiece. But the object is made problematic by the camera at the same time that Igor gazes at Assita through the hole in the wall. Filmed through the fabric, the image imposes a blurry texture that deprives us of a clear view. As Marks explains, a fetish's real power does not derive from the distant appreciation (as in the "fetishizing gaze"), but from contact: "the feather of a sacrificial chicken is a sacred fetish because the chicken is sacred; the relics of saints, preserved fingers or scraps of cloth, gain their value as a fetish through contact with the saint" (Marks 2000, 56). The film points to this tactile way of giving value to things when Assita forbids Igor to touch the statuette when the two thugs break it: "leave it alone, don't touch," she says.

We can excavate a partial or situational meaning from this object by piecing together its touch history in the film. At one important moment the statuette comes into contact with two other objects, a radio and, perhaps not coincidentally, a chicken. These objects also have a history, for both of them have come into contact with Hamidou at the moment of his death. The radio in part caused his death, since it was while reaching for the radio that Hamidou slipped from the scaffold. The chicken touches Hamidou's corpse immediately afterward when Assita, not suspecting her husband's demise, chases it through the courtyard as

Hamidou lay under a discarded door. It even hops onto the door before Roger chases it away. The connection with the statuette comes a few days later, when Igor finds the radio in an abandoned stairwell and returns it to Assita's room.

When Igor arrives, Assita opens the door in a shot that foregrounds Igor's head in the hallway looking inside at her, reluctant to cross the threshold forbidden by his father. On a table in the background, between them in the image, sits the statuette, jumping to the viewer's attention (figure 10). Again deep space and surface are confounded, leaving a haptic plane on which we are invited to read the image. Inside, we cut to a close-up of the boy, and then pan with his gaze across the room to Assita's face: wallpaper, brightly colored towels, and fabrics stand out from the wall. The camera follows her gaze down to the radio (over the thick texture of her woolen sweater) until the camera momentarily frames it and the statuette on the table next to her. It then pans its way back up Assita's arm to her face when suddenly she glares at Igor; it quickly follows her gaze over to him, somewhat behind her glance, and back to her when he asks what the matter is. This *plan séquence* shot is entirely dictated by the bodies and glances of the actors, locking our eyes into their intimate relation and giving texture to their space.

Figure 10. The statuette on the haptic plane. |

The touch history accumulates layers. There is then an unprepared cutaway, of six seconds, to a clucking chicken and Assita's hands reaching for it. We must be in the courtyard. The cut back to the room shows a close-up of the chicken at the moment Assita's knife enters it. We observe her reading in the bird's entrails—again shown closely in the image—and Igor grows nervous as Assita announces her husband is close by, according to the bird's guts. The camera thus links Igor, Assita, statuette, radio, chicken, and finally Hamidou's dead body in a circuit of contact. Igor's nervousness foreshadows his physical reaction when he later accompanies Assita to the home of an elderly diviner. Amazingly, the diviner reads in some cowry shells the presence of an "angry ancestor" who has died far from home and who has not had a proper burial. By this point in the film Igor has become so affected by the uncanny power of objects that he becomes physically uncomfortable, almost ill. Finally, near the end of the film, Assita allows Igor to repair the broken figure, thus acknowledging his place in a history they now share. In this space, disconnected from both the history of the workers' movements and Assita's past, we watch as Igor enters a new history, one with an unclear but real future.

The Dardennes' new style brings the viewer into a close contact with fictional characters, but, perhaps just as important, it also reminds us not to lose sight of our own autonomy. In a dramatic camera effect, the end of the film emphasizes precisely that which separates the viewer from the fictional world. As Assita, Tiga, and Igor disappear into the tunnel, the camera, for the first time, does not pursue (figure 11). Not only does it stop advancing, but it remains unadjusted as the three exit the field of focus. The image goes abruptly dark (though the sound of the passing trains remains) and the credits start to roll. Often students watching the film wonder what will happen now, beyond their time with the characters, a question that ineluctably leads them to discuss Igor's familial situation, the political situation, and connections between the situation and their world. The film begins to take root in the spectator's personal life.

Despite our hypotheses, Assita and Igor are fictional characters who have no real future after the end of the film. But we are not: Our lives go on, and it is in this future that we can observe others, and even speak. After ninety minutes of intense empathy with the world of the

Figure 11. Igor and Assita walking away. |

film, this last image sends the viewer back to his or her own experience, outside the movie house. This leaves a contradictory effect, for the film has induced our sensuous involvement without supplying our senses with an object more solid than light and shadow. Their camera plays on an oscillation between presence and absence. Indeed, the term *haptic* suggests this paradox of a sensuous or embodied experience of a film while avoiding the term *tactile,* which would imply an actual, and thus satisfied, touch. Since touch seems to demand an object, the film can only turn the viewer toward his or her own experience to continue its effect. As Luc Dardenne expresses it, "We feel the rope brush against our throat, wrap around our neck, loosen itself, tighten up again. We won't be freed until the end, when the cord will be cut, leaving its marks on our body. What beautiful scars!" (L. Dardenne 2008, 23).

This play of proximity and distance redefines cinematic realism, bringing the emphasis away from media specificity and toward the relation between viewer and film. In his journal Luc writes about a "resurrection of the body" in the cinema, thereby calling to mind André Bazin's (1967) famous essay, "On the Ontology of the Photographic Image," in which Bazin argues that the preservation or embalmment of the body has motivated the evolution of the plastic arts. Bazin makes no secret that he sees in photography and film a "magic" power to capture time, thus satisfying a deep psychological need to resist death (see Bazin 1967). For the Dardennes, however, this resurrection answers to a different need, one that they find articulated in Bazin's writings as well. Luc Dardenne cites an essay by Bazin praising Jean Renoir's manner of *framing,* which does not enclose an object—as does the frame of a painting—but which excludes other parts of space, suggesting continuity beyond what it encloses. Likewise, the Dardennes hope to see the frames of their films "lost in matter" (L. Dardenne 2008, 22). The frame is thus a *spatial* but not a *visible* continuum that stretches into the always well-developed *hors-champ* (perhaps even into our own experience). The world is there, even if we cannot see it except when it comes within the frame as the camera operator moves through it. As Sarah Cooper lucidly points out, this "resurrection of the body" is not a question of mortality, as it seems to be for Bazin, but of relation, of *morality* or ethics (see Cooper 2007). Instead of trying to bridge the distance between self and other through technique, the brothers now accept it, as if the window no longer clouded their view, but provided the precious possibility of an intense encounter. The body-camera doesn't seek to "fix" the reality of the world in an immortal image, but to determine a point of contact with it even as it moves. Despite their eschewal of classic means of framing and editing, the Dardennes do not simply resort to "irrational" cuts and shots; indeed, their style is quite rigorously structured, but according to other concerns than action and story: The movie theater becomes an ethical space.

The Dardennes make films about political issues, few of which are more polarizing than undocumented immigration. But they do so differently than do most overtly political or ideological filmmakers. Martin O'Shaughnessy appropriately associates the brothers with other 1990s French realists (including Erick Zonca—*La vie rêvée des anges,* 1998; Manuel Poirier—*Western,* 1997; and Robert Guédiguian—*Marius et Jeannette,* 1997; and that would include the *cinéma de banlieue*) who have taken a renewed interest in social and political problems.[7] One criticism of these films that O'Shaughnessy considers before rejecting it as "churlish" is that they uselessly reflect the incapacity of any oppositional tactic in a global economy that has totally disenfranchised the institutions through which workers have historically shown opposition. It is true that there is no "overarching language of opposition" in the Dardenne films (O'Shaughnessy 2005, 77). It is true that, from *La promesse* on, there will be no large group scenes of communities and strikes. Instead, the brothers do something more pressing and useful; they evoke, and perhaps produce, solidarity through a combination of perceptual empathy and rational conversation. The proof of the pudding is in the eating. The depth of the scars left by *La promesse* shows in the transformation of these inconspicuous local filmmakers whose careers were ending into minor, critical global artists. In addition to awards from the Los Angeles Film Critics Association, the Seattle Society of Film Critics, the Iranian Fajr film festival, and numerous other prizes, it has been a counter-circuit favorite. Its power to affect politically minded people remains twelve years later, as it makes its Brazilian premiere in the 2008 festival *Clandestina Liberdade,* whose theme is immigration in the contemporary world.

Budget and Rhythm

In the process of making *La promesse* and their next film, *Rosetta* (1999), the Dardennes developed a revealing and exceptionally consistent *modus operandi* that they have loosely followed to make their subsequent films. The process begins, out of necessity because of the two heads, with dialogue about a screenplay—"We talk, we talk, we talk" (Dardenne 2008, 33)—often inspired by something the brothers have witnessed or read about, a crime, a story told by a friend, or a person seen in the streets of Seraing. A numbered outline emerges, with some fifty points, listing actions, spaces, situations, and dialogues. A working title comes out of one of the points. The title is an essential organizing principle for the brothers' thinking, but it usually changes several times as emphasis shifts during the writing phase. In his diary entries about the 2005 film *The Child,* Luc names at least four alternative titles. Luc, who has also taught a screenwriting workshop in Brussels since just after *Falsch,* then writes a first draft, followed by more conversations, more drafts, until the sixth or seventh draft has been completed. At that point the screenplay is given to one or a few close friends. The brothers have given "screenplay assistant" credit to the critic and documentary maker Léon Michaux on *La promesse* and *Rosetta.* Later their favored collaborator will be one of their coproducers, Denis Freyd.

The mention of Denis Freyd indicates just how singular the Dardennes' process is in the context of contemporary French—and Belgian—cinema. Freyd is a well-respected producer in France and a member of the Club des 13, a group of screen professionals—ranging from screenwriters to producers to exporters—who have written a highly critical report (Club des 13 2008) on the quality of French cinema—*Le milieu n'est plus un pont mais une faille* (*The Middle Is No Longer a Bridge, but a Fault Line*). By "the middle," the group means a long tradition of well-made, medium-budget films (small by American standards, between 3 and 8 million euros), which has made French cinema an important world cinema. The Club maintains that not only is the number of such films on the decline (though not as quickly as one might expect) but that their quality has gone dramatically downhill as well. According to the report, the main problems are caused by the multiple financial partners required to make a film of the middle today. This means multiple voices, often with contradictory interests, beginning with the screenplay, which sometimes undergoes many last-minute rewritings. Botched screenplays lead to halfhearted directing efforts, to too much control by actors, and, finally, to bad films.

The Dardennes (whose recent films fall on the lower end of the middle in terms of budget) show that, with a strong dose of obduracy, it is still possible to make exceptional films of the middle. Again like Truffaut, whose Films du Carrosse allowed him the freedom to break from the traditions of the late 1950s, the brothers have insisted on remaining the delegated producers of all their films and have not had to compromise their vision. Their budgets have actually increased over the years: In 2002, *The Son* cost as much to make as *Thinking of You*, even though the latter was made with trendy actors, contained complex crowd scenes, and was filmed on 35mm stock while the former was made with relative unknowns, shot with a simple handheld camera, and filmed in 16mm (see Sojcher 2005, 171). The budget has increased in the most precious line item for a film of the middle—time. Each Dardenne film since *La promesse* has been years in preparation, usually with three years between releases, though each screenplay is in the works well before the preceding film's release. This also allows the brothers to spend months on preparation, scouting locations with their DV camera, while acting out the scenes themselves in order to explore spaces.

Casting and preparation of the actors also requires more time than in a traditional production. The brothers often advertise in newspapers, sort through the hundreds of photographs and résumés they receive, before auditioning dozens of unknowns. Wardrobe and accessories are chosen often by the brothers themselves, in dialogue with the actors, during long conversations about the characters. They work with the actors for weeks before the shoot.

Part of the budget also goes toward keeping the various locations in preparation and keeping the crew and actors available for the entire shoot. Though this is a habit learned while filming *Falsch,* when the brothers had a very limited time to film in the airport, it now allows the fastidious brothers to retake scenes as new problems arise. Doing so is especially useful since the film is shot in continuity. Editing takes place in late winter and spring, meaning the film is ready just in time for the festival circuit. The afterlife of the films has also settled into a certain rhythm. They have all been shown in competition at Cannes, where they have yet to fail to win some award (most recently the screenplay award for *Le silence de Lorna,* 2008), a critical recognition essential to distribution and the financing of the next project. The brothers are also sensitive to the need to promote the film so that it finds its audience and have given generous interviews. This says much about their tactics. Working both within and without the system, they are able to create with freedom but maintain a relevance that allows their work to have an impact. By the time the film is released, usually in late summer or early fall and the following spring in North America, it is time to actively pursue the next project, which will likewise be personally overseen from the original idea to the DVD rights.

Rosetta and Émilie Dequenne

By the end of the four years it took to make *La promesse,* the brothers were ready to tackle a variety of subjects and fine-tune their method. With *Rosetta,* the situation is economic. The heroine of the title is an unskilled, seventeen-year-old, unemployed girl; but through her story, which Luc calls the "portrait of an époque," the film taps into the employment malaise of 1990s Europe (L. Dardenne 2008, 86). In 1998, the year *Rosetta* was shot, more than half of Belgians under 25 years old had not found a job six months after finishing their schooling, with the worst numbers in French-speaking Wallonia. The types of career young people could expect had also degraded, with the highest increases in jobs coming in low-paying, unskilled industries such as the so-called HORECA (hotel, restaurant, and café) industries in which Rosetta works. Rosetta works in a food-processing plant, but at the beginning of the film she has just been, in the euphemistic language of the personnel office, "thanked" [*remerciée*]. While making the film, the Dardennes referred to her as "le surnuméraire," or the "overstaffed." The reason given for her dismissal is just a pretext; for her supervisor makes clear that she has been let go because she has finished her "*période d'essai,*" at which time she must either be hired permanently (and paid more, with benefits) or fired.

But *Rosetta* is also a film about an actress. At Cannes *Rosetta* received the first of the brothers' *palmes d'or* for best picture and a best actress award for Émilie Dequenne. Her award, which she shared with another nonprofessional (Séverine Caneele in Bruno Dumont's *L'Humanité*), even stirred up a mild controversy as some commentators took the jury's decision as a slight to the professional actresses with more traditional training who had entered films that year (see Schmitt 1999 and Austin 2004). There is something appropriate about the association of the two prizes, for Dequenne's sheer corporeal presence dictates the style of the film, from *mise-en-scène* to the camera movement. Her performance borders on the athletic. The shooting schedule itself seems often to be driven by ensuring the least comfort possible for the actors. In the three-year rhythm, shooting begins in late fall, starting usually in October and continuing into winter, making for very long three-month shoots. Underdressed, cold, and sometimes doused in water, Dequenne's unmade-up cheeks are rosy from the pumping blood and her hands are yellow from the lack of circulation to her extremities. Her various battles (including extracting herself from a muddy lake and lugging her mother up a set of stairs) are feats of strength. Typically the Dardennes force their actors to run through scenes innumerable times so that they are at the brink of exhaustion when the takes become serious.

The collaboration with Dequenne is exemplary of the brothers' approach to actors. This approach has ripened over the years, and its seed can be detected in Bruno Crémer's advice during the filming of *Falsch* that an actor should be thought of as a body moving through space. Over time the brothers have increasingly explored their actors less as mask wearers or characters but as physical bodies. Actors in this state are no longer thinking about their careers, but giving something of themselves (figure 12). Between Dequenne and Rosetta there is little difference, as the abstract character gives way constantly to the physical presence of the actress. Such an approach is not exactly flattering to the vanities of actors. By capturing Dequenne in her physical suffering, fatigue, without the delicacies of makeup, and with little concern for showing her best side, the camera does not give her exposure only in a sense positive for actors. In ways described by George Toles, it is exposure of weakness, fatigue, ugliness, and mortality. Perhaps too often associated with immortality and redemption in the film theories of a Bazin or a Kracauer, photography and film can really "oscillate excitingly between the possibilities of a saving disclosure and a humiliating betrayal" (Toles 2001, 235). Much of *Rosetta*'s power resides in this ambiguity.

Through redemption or betrayal, the camera in *Rosetta* is wholly concerned with the body and face of Émilie Dequenne. In framing the girl, the Dardennes were again inspired by Johan Van der Keuken, whom they had met just after finishing *Falsch*. Luc Dardenne writes

Figure 12. Dequenne on the set.

about a scene from Van der Keuken's *Nouvel âge glacial* involving a young ice-cream factory worker resembling Rosetta, who tries to read a love letter. As the illiterate girl begins struggling with each syllable, the camera begins to pan nervously around her room, as if the image were bumping into the walls at the rhythm of the girl's hesitations. "The gaze of the filmmaker has been called to by the distress of the person filmed. From that plea the shot is born, a unique and entirely new form that would never have existed otherwise" (L. Dardenne 2008, 178).

Once again the brothers took great care selecting the camera, a smaller 16mm instead of 35mm, which was chosen to better film the many fast-moving following shots of the actress as she dashes through the film. It was this hypermobile handheld camera—Jean-Michel Frodon called it "the mad camera" [la caméra folle]—which struck viewers and critics at the time (Frodon 1999b). Unlike *La promesse,* which followed a few characters in their interactions with each other, *Rosetta* follows just one character throughout. Nobody and really nothing else shares the frame with her. Space is distended, alienated from her, and unlike many realistic filmmakers, the Dardennes rarely exploit depth of field. Seraing begins to move further off screen; Rosetta is not detached, but her story could take place in any disaffected urban setting, and the continual filming in this place seems attached more to the Dardennes' personal experience than to a desire to document the city. Instead, the camera moves in to encounter the person. It is positioned closer, and a medium-angle lens slightly distorts the people and objects that appear in the background, an effect increased by the 16 to 35mm blowup. Especially striking are the numerous close-ups of Dequenne's face, the unique form into which the frame melts and which we examine close enough that its textures and contours become familiar—the moles on her cheek or the dark peach fuzz that grows high on her cheekbones.

The goal of this camera is to follow this compound being composed of actress and character, Émilie Dequenne and Rosetta. After the soundless credits, a sudden clanking strikes the viewer's ears, without an initial visual object to attach it to, like an explosion in a battle scene. The camera, inside a corridor, picks up in extreme close-up a door that is already being opened (thus explaining the bang). The camera seems to have been minding its own business when the film begins; but it immediately swings up to show the back of a young woman, dressed in a white coat and wearing a hairnet. The film is thus born out of this startled look at Rosetta, already trying to catch a glimpse of her without knowing where she is going or why. A machine-gun-quick series of following shots show Rosetta running down corridors and stairs, each ending in an abrupt cut as the girl slams a door in our face or ducks past a machine, behind some boxes or under a conveyor belt. Finally she arrives in a locker room, where she confronts a coworker: "Is it true that you said I'm always late?" When a supervisor catches up to her, we see her face for the first time; it is determined, demanding an explanation of him now, unblinking. Rosetta punches him in the stomach, and bedlam results. Shots are not purposely distorted, or canted, nor are they noticeably taken from strange angles. If they lack balance, it is because of the speed at which Rosetta moves and the difficulties of the operator in keeping up. By the end of this scene, the operator seems to give up on following, the camera stops moving, and we see only the white jackets flying around in complete anarchy. It ends with an emotionally juiced Rosetta breathing heavily, like a soldier after a particularly intense skirmish.

We viewers also have a moment of respite; but just when we think the scene is over, it turns out to have only begun. Another cut brings us again to Rosetta running, this time a blurry policeman on her tail, as she tries various escape routes before locking herself in a bathroom. When two policemen drag her out, she claws with hands and feet, even dragging a bulky row of lockers behind her. The film is no longer making a point about how much Rosetta wants a job; it is trying to keep up with Émilie Dequenne—at the limits of her strength. Already this scene gives an idea of what the Dardennes mean when they say that the narrative is even "less articulated" than in *La promesse*. "We were not trying to recount a story," writes Dardenne, "but to describe the action of someone whose entire being is obsessed with existing normally, with being part of society, with no longer being excluded, with not disappearing" (L. Dardenne 2008, 72). The screenplay spells out several details: Rosetta works in a frozen food plant; the woman she confronts is working at a computer screen; the supervisor is punched in the stomach and face; Rosetta spits in his direction, and so on. Some of this transpires, some of it doesn't, but here as elsewhere the *mise-en-scène* and the lack of camera distance will not let us hash out these details. Instead our perspective is entirely and helplessly within the movement of bodies.

Rosetta's battles evoke an unexpected genre. When the critic Thierry Jobin (1999) called Rosetta a "little Rambo in a synthetic skirt and mustard colored tights," Jean-Pierre Dardenne replied rather graciously, "We told ourselves right away that *Rosetta* would be a war film, so Rambo, why not?" Daily life in the film takes an uncanny resemblance to war; banal sounds become explosions, ordinary actions demand extraordinary prowess. The film concentrates on the pursuit of basic needs—food, water, shelter, and clothing—and the great effort it requires. Rosetta lives with her mother in a trailer on a campsite; fills her jerrican with water from an outdoor pump; washes her clothes in a plastic bucket; carries a water bottle that she opens with her teeth like a canteen; hides her boots in a drainpipe in the woods. Her resourcefulness is illustrated in innumerable details, such as when she insulates her window against a draft by shoving toilet paper in its cracks or invents a fish trap. Her movements give the film its rhythm, whether she is in a furious battle, marching through the city, or hiding in rare respite.

The camera obsessively follows her actions. A number of shots follow Rosetta as she works her way across the lanes of a periphery highway like an obstacle course, avoiding the speeding cars, moving from urban to wild landscape. She gathers her boots from under a culvert and blazes a trail across the thickets before sneaking into the ironically named "grand canyon" (the campsite). This natural setting could be quite beautiful, the trees in the background have an airy quality that announces the forest at the end of *The Son.* But Rosetta does not seem calmed; rather, she listens for dangerous sounds on the wind, like the arrival of the camp superintendent who might find her poaching trout in the lake.

The film's other characters can be divided into those who have their places in the economic system—the personnel directors she speaks with, the saleswomen at second-hand stores, the boss of the chain of waffle stands (played by Gourmet)—or those like her, camping out "in the hole," as she says. Family does not constitute ties in this jungle. Rosetta's mother—a character conceived in part after interviews with a therapist from Alcoholics Anonymous—moves in the vicious cycle of self-defeating behavior typical of long-term addicts. She lies about drinking, spends Rosetta's rent money on alcohol, and gives the superintendent oral sex instead of paying rent. She has even planted bushes around their camper, accepting her abject existence as a permanent home. At one point Rosetta berates her for accepting the charity of a fish while she has been working so hard catching them in the lake. During their struggle, the second intense battle scene in the film, Rosetta's mother draws a knife. This time Rosetta escapes and throws her mother's bushes in the garbage. But her mother will try to kill her again when Rosetta attempts to commit her to a rehabilitation center, this time by shoving her into the murky lake. Her pleas of "Maman! Maman!" are ignored and she must fish herself out.

One begins to perceive in the Dardennes' work a blossoming if somewhat belated *cinéphilie.* In *La promesse* there were already clear resemblances between the rubble-laden landscape of Rossellini's postwar Berlin in *Germany Year Zero* and postindustrial Seraing. There are also common points with characters in John Ford's films (in *Au dos de nos images,* Luc mentions the impact of *Cheyenne Autumn,* 1964, and *The Man Who Shot Liberty Valence,* 1962), characters who realize they have been part of a system that has denied the rights of others and who are struggling to become ethical agents. Frodon sees in the mobile camera the influence of a number of filmmakers, some from the past, such as Cassavetes (whose *Killing of a Chinese Bookie,* 1977, left traces on *La promesse*) or various new wave filmmakers, some more contemporary, such as Lars von Trier (Frodon 1999a).

With *Rosetta,* one can point to Chaplin's *City Lights* or Pasolini's *Accatone* (also an influence on *The Child*), but, most directly, Robert Bresson's *Mouchette* (1967). This lake, for example, into which Rosetta is thrown, is one of many references to Bresson's film, whose very title seems echoed by *Rosetta.* Bresson's tragic story follows another outsider wandering through muddy landscapes, this time in the north of France. Bresson's is an extremely pessimistic, almost nihilistic film. Mouchette (Nadine Nortier) is persecuted at school, beaten by her alcoholic father, raped during a night spent in the woods, and witness to the death of her sick mother. She kills herself at the end of the film by rolling down a hill and falling into a muddy pond, filmed with a tuft of winter-dormant grass growing at its edge, just like the lake in *Rosetta.* Rosetta's resemblance to Mouchette, however, is complex, often inverted. Here, for example, we are only midway through the film, and Rosetta has been thrown into the pond by another. Rosetta's reaction is to struggle and extricate herself from the mud, which she eventually manages to do. Rosetta resists victimhood, fights for her future.

But Rosetta can resist only by embracing her solitude, and if she fills the frame of the Dardennes' camera, it is because she is alone in the *mise-en-scène* of her life. Besides her mother, Rosetta has no perceivable past at all, and even less a grand history of Belgian labor. And despite the fact that she finally lands a job at a waffle stand, *Rosetta* is an extraordinarily "un-Belgian" film. Beer and waffles are all anyone orders—not the beer and waffles of the Brussels tourist stands, signifiers of a quaint national difference, but just beer and waffles, unhealthy sustenance. With no identifications there is a complete lack of solidarity. She can muster the resources of her physical strength only in a brutal game of musical chairs, with everyone vying for the few places available in the ultraliberal economy (Camhi 1999). The Dardennes include many instances of people "taking the place" of others (L. Dardenne 2008, 78). During her training session, a young mother, the worker whose place she has taken, walks into the kitchen and asks for an unemployment form. In a brief dialogue we learn of her firing after too many days' absence—a narrative that could fill another Dardenne movie. For a moment Rosetta and the woman are alone; Rosetta resists making eye contact through an uncomfortable silence, literally refusing to acknowledge the victim of her success. She accepts the market for what it is, a dehumanized competition in which individuals and their circumstances count for little. It is unsurprising that, when she loses the job a few days later to the boss's son, who has been expelled from school, nobody raises a fuss for her.

The only other important character in the film is Riquet (Fabrizio Rongione), a young man who operates one of the boss's waffle châteaux in the city and who has tipped Rosetta off about the job opening. Riquet is an enigmatic character whose motivations are never explained—we rarely really see him, since the camera is so locked into Rosetta's character. Originally conceived as a seducer, his sexual intentions faded with each draft of the screenplay, as it became less and less possible to imagine Rosetta open to seduction. The brothers admit to having trouble on the set answering Fabrizio Rongione when he pestered them with questions about how to play the character (L. Dardenne 2008, 90). The camera concentrates so stubbornly on Rosetta that Riquet must constantly fade into the background like all the other secondary characters. They finally settled on two pieces of advice. The first was simply to "be there" [être là], the second was "to wait." Riquet is waiting, simply existing there, as Luc says, for a Rosetta "who is not yet there," who refuses the touch of the other. Riquet, in other words, can become a real character only in a story when Rosetta shows up: He is a *potential* friend and lover, but one cannot pierce through her defenses. To wait attentively, as Riquet and we the viewers do, means to dwell in a present with the hope that Rosetta may have a future.

Often, in this cinema about working people "faced with extinction," the future is expressed through basic biology: Will the species reproduce? The child for the Dardennes, as in Levinas's philosophy of fecundity, represents first the erotic relation to the other, and through this relation it represents the future, the continuation of one's self, albeit in another form, in a generation to come (for more on fecundity, see Levinas 1969, 267–69). The erotic becomes a major, but profoundly subterranean, theme in the film, a subject that most commentators neglect perhaps because it seems so foreign to Rosetta's character. This is again like Bresson's Mouchette, a fourteen-year-old, who is just becoming romantically curious when sexual intercourse is inflicted upon her. Bresson often frames Mouchette suggestively, while she is pulling up her stockings or bent over with her bottom in the air, even during the suicide scene. His cruel point is that Mouchette's sexuality is destined to victimization, and until things change, she is in a sense right to take herself out of the cycle of life: She has no future.

Rosetta, who wears stockings eerily similar to Mouchette's, is also filmed in situations that could have an erotic charge. Her own view of sexuality may be darkened by her revulsion at her mother's sexual escapades: "All you think of is drinking and fucking," Rosetta reproaches her. In one scene, after discovering her mother once again exchanging sex for drink, Rosetta storms out of the camper, only to encounter Riquet arriving to tell her about the job opening in the waffle kitchen. His timing is unfortunate, for as he dismounts his moped, she furiously throws herself on him, knocking him to the ground and pounding him with her fists. They struggle, her skirt flailing in the air, revealing her from the waist down, her underwear showing through her stockings as she wraps her legs around Riquet's torso. A scene like this in many other films would have strong erotic intonations, perhaps ending in an embrace, and yet here it ends only when Riquet tells her about the job; and her yielding could hardly be called tender.

This refused eroticism is even more glaring in light of Dequenne's subsequent career, in which her most important roles have highlighted sensuality, in films such as *Oui mais* . . . (2001), or in Claude Berri's casting of her as an innocent but frank seductress opposite of Jean-Pierre Bacri in *The Housekeeper* (2002). The brothers have often admitted difficulties in filming women, and on the set they called Dequenne's character "Rosetto." But isn't this modesty misleading? If the Dardennes do not represent Dequenne as an eroticized other, it is not because they avoid this element of her persona, but because it is stamped out or aborted by Rosetta. She has, for example, a mysterious recurring cramp in her stomach, apparently related to menstruation but also to the stress of looking for a job. Like a wounded soldier removing shrapnel from his gut, she withdraws behind the blanket that separates her bunk from the rest of the camper and, using a hair dryer, heats up her belly to relieve the pain. A close-up pans from her face down her torso to her stomach in a shot that again would be erotic if she weren't in so much pain. These mysterious cramps are made only more ambiguous by Luc's description of them as "birthing pains that deliver no child" (L. Dardenne 2008, 91). Rosetta's body is at ease only with the metallic tools of her job in the waffle kitchen: Filling a large mixing bowl with flour and eggs, and then holding two bottles of milk under her arms and pouring them in, she is serene and maternal.

The Dardennes examine this erotic turmoil in an extremely touching scene inflected with a subtle (though very mixed) comedy (figure 13). When Rosetta drops in unannounced at Riquet's apartment (she can't bear the idea of going home to her mother), another film might consider the stage set for seduction. And yet, try as he does, Riquet cannot make the slightest impression on Rosetta. Rongione, evoking Chaplin, combines earnestness and physical humor as an endearing failure. He first gives Rosetta a tour of a dilapidated storage room that she could rent from his landlady, pointing at a pile of broken doors in a corner and declaring "and here you have a shower." Meanwhile Rosetta has been eying with envy an old pair of rubber boots (she had, after all, lost hers when her mother threw her in the pond). Riquet slyly offers

Figure 13. Rosetta and Riquet having dinner.

a beer; but she takes water. They stand awkwardly in his kitchen, their silence making the everyday noises of the apartment fill the air, until Rosetta notices a trophy on a mantelpiece. Riquet brags about being a gymnastics champion; but he has a hard time impressing her when he can't quite get a simple handstand right, and falls painfully on his back. They share a brief giggle. Over a dinner of french toast, Rosetta finally takes a beer, which she chugs down in one draft before a dumbstruck Riquet. He then makes small talk about music and asks whether Rosetta would like to hear a tape of his band. He is a completely incompetent drummer, and the loud tape drones on for minutes as they sit staring at their food. Finally the band kicks in, and he forces Rosetta to dance, at least when everyone picks up the beat again after he bungles the beat. The music captivates Riquet, but Rosetta is very uncomfortable and seems on the edge of tears. This kind of touch and movement are wholly alien to her and Riquet must peel her arms away from her body. She has another painful cramp and rushes out of the apartment. Perhaps in another film this scene would be the stuff of romantic comedy; here it is pure anguish and paralysis.

Chaplin haunts many scenes in this film, and the brothers' long-standing love for the Little Tramp is confirmed, for example, in their discussion of *Modern Times* that appears as a bonus feature on the American DVD version. But Rosetta is a *Charlot* who has replaced the humor of physical movement with an embodied shame. Like Chaplin in *City Lights* (1931), she wants desperately to be a member of society. Instead she is a pariah.

Dardenne also cites Hannah Arendt's description of the pariah: "But he who, like the pariah, is sent away [*congédié*] by society cannot think himself as relieved of the situation [*tiré d'affaire*] (despite the judgment) since society continues to assert that it is real and tends to make him believe that he is unreal, that he is nobody" (L. Dardenne 2008, 71). The banished one thus continually wonders whether she truly exists. A few moments after dashing out of Riquet's apartment, Rosetta returns (to pick up the forgotten boots) and asks whether she can sleep on his couch. The camera moves in close to Rosetta's face, as she suddenly and eerily begins to speak to herself, and then to respond. "Your name is Rosetta—My name is Rosetta. You have found a job—I have found a job. You have found a friend—I have found a friend. You have a normal life—I have a normal life. You will not fall in the hole—I will not fall in the hole" (figure 14). This scene is reminiscent of the superb moments in Lars von Trier's *Breaking the Waves* (1996), in which Emily Watson as

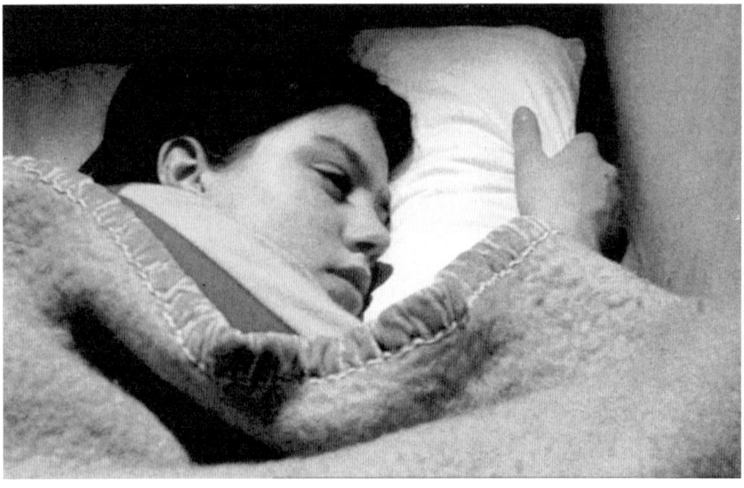

Figure 14. Je m'appelle Rosetta. |

Bess converses with God in a country church, first speaking in her voice, then answering in His. As with Bess, one begins to question Rosetta's sanity. Unlike Bess, however, whose face is brightly lit and who speaks with the conviction that God is listening to her (indeed, God actually fulfills his every promise to her), Rosetta is alone and in the dark, speaking in total self-alienation, almost schizophrenically trying to convince herself that she exists.

This fragile self-image is instantly wiped out and her happiness brutally shattered when she loses her job to her boss's son. Even though the boss has promised to give her back a job as soon as he has an opening, she again fights, starts beating the boy, and clings to a sack of flour as if it were a dead loved one. Jobless again, Rosetta falls to new lows of desperation, in which she will attempt anything to regain her spot. The film unfolds on no less than three distinct moments, each of which could easily constitute the end of her story. At each moment, the camera concentrates on Rosetta's face—evoking again Levinas's ethical face-to-face situations—in important close-ups.

The first possible ending suggests betrayal and, nearly, murder. The import of her boss's promise is that Rosetta merely needs one of her coworkers to disappear to gain back her job. She gives a hint of how far she will go when Riquet comes to see her at the Grand Canyon. His arrival surprises her while she is checking her fishing lines, and she is obliged to quickly toss a hooked fish back into the pond. Always eager to help, he holds her hand and stoops over the water to retrieve the line, but she slips and lets him fall (more evocations of the "suicide" scene in *City Lights*). But instead of helping him, she runs behind some bushes while Riquet calls her name—drawing a correspondence between her and her alcoholic mother. The camera remains fixed on her face as we listen to Riquet's increasingly desperate calls. Having been there herself, she must know exactly how he feels. At the last moment, she does fish him out, but even the dense Riquet seems to notice her slowness to act.

In earlier versions of the screenplay, the Dardennes considered having Rosetta actually commit murder here. Instead, she commits the social equivalent. Already she had noticed a waffle iron in Riquet's apartment and deduced that he has been selling waffles on his own from the stand's supplies, pilfering from their boss. When she betrays him, Riquet is immediately fired, in her presence, and the job falls to her.

She has found a place. A few scenes later we see Rosetta in medium close-up, content, standing inside the waffle stand wearing Riquet's old apron. The Dardennes again use the off-screen space and the image of Rosetta's face to full advantage: We hear customer after customer ordering waffles and beer while the camera shows Rosetta's contented smile as she collects their money and doles out change, moving comfortably in the flow of the economy. But she does not exactly interact with these people. She can have a dialogue onscreen only with herself, as the onscreen is here determined by the exclusion of others. She even ties the door to the stand closed with a wire just in case someone should try to violate that space. In his review, Jean-Michel Frodon explains that he would have preferred the film to end on this contented smile and the cautionary tale it tells: A heartless society makes heartless individuals; war isn't pretty.

The second potential ending bears a no less pessimistic message. Its seed is planted in this scene at the waffle wagon, for at the end of it we recognize one of those voices—Riquet's—as it again penetrates Rosetta's onscreen space. After work Riquet harasses her, follows her around an overpass on his whining moped and then blocking her way on foot, asking her a simple question: "Why did you do that?" Behind them we catch glimpses of the Meuse. Rosetta can only answer that she wanted to let him die in the pond. But Riquet reminds her that she helped him anyway. Rosetta can only flee Riquet, preserve her solitude. But as a final reminder that she is not alone, Rosetta arrives home to find her mother passed out drunk in the grass. With great effort, she lugs her across the campground to their camper, drags her up the stairs, and dumps her in bed. She then fills a pan with water from her jerrican, starts a fire, and plops in an egg. The camera lingers on this egg sitting in the water, and then pans slowly up to Rosetta's inscrutable face. As the egg cooks, she walks to the camp telephone, calls her boss, and quits her job. Back in the camper, she peels the egg, turns on the gas, climbs into bed, and waits to die. She only glances briefly and unsentimentally at her mother before pulling over the blanket that separates her bunk. We watch her again in close-up, eating and listening, for well over a minute, to the hissing of the gas valve off-screen again, and we fully expect her to die, exhausted and as hardened and closed-in as this egg.

Both these scenes reflect what Luc Dardenne calls "a certain sadism in [their] gaze" (L. Dardenne 2008, 70). They both present a morally bankrupt and futureless world. Both also have plenty of cinematic antecedents. *Mouchette,* for example, offers a negative portrait of humanity and is one of the strongest examples of what one could call a sadistic style. Nothing can save Mouchette from victimization, and most view her suicide more as deliverance than tragedy. Bruno Dumont and Michael Haneke may be Bresson's most direct heirs in this sense. At times such filmmakers seem to punish viewers with the suffering of others.

Let's follow this visual sadism to its harshest degree in *Rosetta.* In another topsy-turvy Chaplinesque moment, the pitch coming from the gas valve suddenly rises and becomes airy: Rosetta, out of fuel, has botched even her suicide. But she *still* won't give up: pulling on her boots, she hauls her empty tank across the campground, gives the superintendent a token, and begins to lug the new one back to the camper. Several times during this brutal sequence (the shot lasts more than four minutes) she has to stop because she cannot bear its weight. Quietly at first, behind Rosetta's heavy breathing, we begin to hear the bleating of Riquet's moped and then see him arrive, anger written on his face, as he drives around her tauntingly. She stops her herculean effort to throw gravel at him, to chase him and his judgmental gaze away. Eventually she can no longer support her burden. She drops the tank and tumbles upon it, sobbing and rocking her face back and forth on it like an infant seeking comfort from a favorite blanket. By showing Rosetta in such utter abjection the Dardennes give us a particularly strong version of what George Toles has termed a "humiliation scene," in which we are taken "to the edge of what we can bear to witness of another's writhing in shame" (Toles 2001, 237). Rosetta is humiliated in her refusal of the touch of others, in her reliance on her own strength, which finally falters.

It is in conveying this humiliation that the convergence of the brothers' camera style, the ethical story, and the contribution of the actress becomes acutely effective. Toles talks about a good photo "surprising its object" (Toles 2001, 236). Dequenne is not presented here as someone acting a role, but as someone suffering. This last sequence shot was repeated dozens of times, and the exhaustion on Dequenne's face, traditionally the privileged object of our emotional response, is real. And the close attention paid to Dequenne through the film makes us perceive its coloring, yellow with cold, red with tears, in an exceptionally strong way. The mask of the character is broken and the real person appears. Fatigue and tears are real. It is an ambitious role because of Dequenne's willingness to expose not a character but herself in such an abject state before the camera and the public view. Her subsequent roles prove well enough that she is not interested in playing the abject in every project, perhaps never again, and that another *Rosetta* may never be possible for her. The camera surprises this humiliation by following her, hunting her down as it were, making the entire film flow out of her body and her face, betraying her in a way that would give most people nightmares.

To what end would the filmmakers choose to humiliate their lead actress? Toles (2001) finishes his thought about the humiliation scene by referring to our "need for a reprieve" (237). Some films hardly give us much to satisfy this need—Bresson and Haneke rarely give us a satisfactory redemption, perhaps thinking it more reflective of society's or mankind's moral condition that way. And yet in his diary, Luc criticizes the cynical perspective. Though speaking of television, his words could apply to much cinema when he says that the cynical conscience "knows that its ideals are better than the reality that they could transform, but it accepts being separated from its ideals. That's how it is! That's reality! Under the pretext of realism, this conscience resigns itself to its unhappiness, and because this arrangement cannot completely dissipate its awareness of unhappiness, it becomes arrogant, mean, full of contempt" (L. Dardenne 2008, 41).

There is thus a hopeful tendency in the Dardennes' work, no more but no less justified than cynicism. Along with the sadistic exposure, the brothers feel a countervailing imperative to shake off resignation and show "the moment when a human being, a character, escapes the grip" of evil (L. Dardenne 2008, 71). It is almost as if contingency takes on the power of the good in this final scene, when the coincidence of the empty gas tank brings Rosetta out to meet Riquet. She is not left to wallow permanently on the ground at his feet: We hear Riquet shut off his moped, and then we see his hand and shoulder helping Rosetta to her feet. The camera moves in to show her face, turning to look, for the first time, at Riquet, without her defenses, and without the armor of her face. On her face one might read guilt and need, both indicating that she recognizes her place in a social relation. But she is not abandoned by Riquet, and the scene answers our need for reprieve. Even though Riquet remains off screen, the shot also reveals the brilliance of his role as a catalyst for Rosetta's ethical character. Patient, frustrated, and angry, he has been waiting, and Rosetta has finally turned toward him. Her egg has cracked, and she has stepped outside; the beginning of a relationship is enough to let the film end without expanding the narrative frame. In *Rosetta,* humiliation is not its own end. This time, now reminiscent of *Modern Times,* there are two characters, a man and a woman, and even if Riquet does not tell Rosetta to smile as Chaplin does at the end of his film, and even if they do not walk arm in arm into the sunset, there is a sense of hope.

The end of the film also presents a discrete act of social rebellion on Rosetta's part. She is no longer the model employee, willing to submit herself to whatever the labor market dictates in order to keep her job. Her humiliation has brought her emancipation—and her act of quitting her job is both an acceptance of personal responsibility and a refusal to work in this system.

But for us viewers, the connection between humiliation and emancipation should give us pause in this "portrait of an époque." Quoting Levinas, the Dardennes claim for their cinema a fundamental point of departure: "spiritual life is essentially moral life, and its realm of predilection is economic" (L. Dardenne 2008, 71). What does it say about the way we live that getting and keeping a job must dehumanize a person? Why does a camera need to do such violence to our normal ways of looking for us to see this? Why should the young feel like pariahs? Why should their desire to be employed tempt them into the morally wrong? Asking such questions plants the seed of solidarity, and when we reenter our own lives and confront problems such as unemployment, we should have a new sensitivity to the faces behind statistics. This seems to have been the effect of the film. In September 1999 the Belgian employment minister, Laurette Onkelinx, a native of Seraing, presented what she called the *plan Rosetta,* legislation that aimed to increase the number of jobs created for young workers just completing their education (see Stroobants 2000). The Dardennes themselves take no credit for the plan, nor do they endorse it when they are asked about it in interviews. One may even question just how effective it has been, for it has been criticized by both employers and unions, who were not consulted when the plan was being crafted (see Eurofound 1999). This fragile solidarity seems appropriate to a film without a past: Starting with the simple acknowledgment of the other, it is not anchored in traditional representative institutions, but in search of new ones.

The Son

> Vous voulez vous battre
> Et vous n'arrivez à vous rencontrer
> Que pour vous frôler
>
> [You want to exchange blows
> But you only succeed in meeting
> To brush against each other]
>
> —Guillevic 1961, 61

Though *The Son* is completely fictional, its crisis is rooted in the tragically real. In early 1993, two ten-year-old boys (referred to as Child A and B during their trial) led two-year-old Jamie Bulger out of a Liverpudlian shopping mall and violently killed him. The intense and sometimes morbid media coverage of the case emphasized the devastation of the Bulger family—the tabloids followed their mourning as well as the parents' divorce and remarriages, but also the anger of the community and cries for recrimination. Once the press had discovered the identities of the two killers—often described as "monsters"—it also examined in detail their families. Both boys came from broken families who were experiencing problems related to alcoholism, paternal abandonment, and poverty—problems found throughout the Dardennes' oeuvre. It was these killers and their families who drew the Dardennes' attention most: "We followed the investigations into the families of these kids, because for us, the question was to know from what one inherited the ability to murder another child at that age. That was a question that haunted us for a rather long time, almost 10 years, and it came back to us very quickly when we began writing this script. There was a sort of reversal, in that instead of following the father of the killer, here it's the father of the murdered boy" (Kehr 2003).

In *The Son*, Olivier Gourmet (in his third role with the Dardennes) plays a father, also named Olivier, whose only son has been murdered five years previously. His life has been traumatically altered: He has divorced, quit his job at a family-owned lumberyard, and, to "feel useful" has become a teacher of carpentry at a rehabilitation center for youthful offenders. At the film's beginning, we see Olivier reading the dossier of a newcomer who wants to enter his class. He recognizes the name of Francis Thirion (Morgan Marinne), the boy who, at the age of eleven, killed his son. Olivier initially refuses to accept the boy into his group, though he doesn't inform anyone of their secret connection. He becomes obsessed with Francis, follows him through the center, and finally gives him a spot in his carpentry group. The camera follows Olivier's hesitations and conflicts in this situation, which seems destined to end poorly. The last third of the film follows Olivier and Francis alone on a tense drive to the remote family lumberyard, where Olivier is tempted to kill.

The Son shares the theme of a dead child with several films of the late 1990s and early 2000s. Emma Wilson, in her study of "cinema's missing children," discusses works that offer "new more or less adequate modes of response to the fear or experience of losing a child" (2003, 3). Concentrating on filmmakers like Bruno Dumont, Atom Egoyan, Pedro Almodovar, Lynne Ramsay, and Nanni Moretti, Wilson excludes from her book genre or Hollywood cinema, which, though good litmus tests for broad cultural tendencies, seems to lack independent cinema's "diagnostic and interrogative power" (3). Wilson refers to just one blockbuster dealing with the theme, Steven Spielberg's *Minority Report* (2002), which came out in France at the same time as *The Son.* Spielberg's film contains an important child-disappearance plot, but the story, as Wilson rightly points out, exploits the situation "to explore the desire for recrimination and revenge." It is about "action rather than reflection" (4). In this respect *Minority Report* shares something with the press coverage of the Bulger case, which has been sensationally rehashed, especially since 2001 when the killers were released under new identities, often with indignant calls for exposing their whereabouts.

Wilson does not mention *The Son* (her book came out shortly after the film), but the film seems to engage more directly with the desire for revenge than most independent films. As Luc told Dave Kehr of the *New York Times,* "the theme of revenge is very ancient. . . . It extends from Greek tragedy to contemporary movies, where revenge often serves as a device to construct scenarios. We wanted to confront this device, to see what you could do with it—how you might be able to escape from vengeance, without being a saint, or to show that human beings might have the capacity to break the pattern of repeating the same murderous gestures" (Kehr 2003).

Luc delves into the theme in his journal as well, through his subtle reading of Shakespeare's *Hamlet.* Hamlet is a young man whose only desire is to flourish, have friends, and love Ophelia, but whose father's ghost refuses to set him free. Hamlet's father imposes an inflexible and sterile law of revenge, something of a cult to the dead (another subject on which Dardenne meditates in the journal), which will only perpetuate the chaos in Denmark. Vengeance is seen by the brothers as a negative impulse that destabilizes society and prevents the continuation of the family line. It is a view that reverberates with the work of René Girard, another thinker whom the Dardennes have mentioned from time to time. Girard, especially in *Violence and the Sacred* (1977) has argued that violent acts proliferate, especially in small societies, as one act instigates a similar response, which in turn demands another response, in an escalation of mimetic violence. Religious and later secular societies reduce violence by funneling it into either an individual sacrificial victim or, in the latter case, the secular law. There are in effect two types of laws: the first is the destructive compulsive law of mimetic revenge; the second, the more humane and reflective law that we obey so that human society may flourish. In his own reading of *Hamlet,* Girard (1990) argues that Hamlet unsuccessfully resists the cycle of violence, and that Shakespeare wrote his tragedy against the revenge plays of his time.

The Son makes no attempt to explain the source of violence, only to examine one way, in a particular social situation, of stemming its tide. Can anything make the father resist the call to avenge his son's death? While writing *The Son,* Luc was also meditating on a passage from Hegel concerning the dialectics of child rearing. Hegel states that parents, as they look at their children, contemplate "their own suppression." This is because, through a process that Hegel calls education, parents instill an independent consciousness in the child, preparing him or her for adulthood and thus as a replacement for themselves (L. Dardenne 2008, 98). Dardenne considers this process an essential step forward, since if parents choose "not to eat their children" (another Cronos reference), the future can take place. Parenthood becomes a willed act of education.

Not only does the cycle of violence end, but the parents find themselves continued into the future both genetically and through the transmission of practices and values; they "die by surviving, retreat from life by prolonging it," as Luc puts it (L. Dardenne 2008, 98). Such a prognosis again echoes Levinas's concept of fecundity, according to which parenthood gives the individual subject an opportunity to extend itself beyond its own death: The child is at once the same and different, a direct relation with the future. Levinas writes, quoting the bible: "My child is a stranger (Isaiah 49), but a stranger who is not only mine, for he is me. He is me a stranger to myself" (Levinas 1969, 267). Our relationship to future generations is thus at once one of responsibility and our own survival. For the Dardennes, hopes for a nonviolent future, especially in the social conditions of working man on the brink of extinction, rely on a transmission of a law or wisdom: As Luc mentions in writing on the Bulger case in *Au dos de nos images*, "what could they have inherited to commit this act? The state of things in our world" (L. Dardenne 2008, 20). What makes the knot of *The Son* so tense is that Olivier is both son and father. He has been bereft of his relation to the future and is in a position of teaching the one who stole it.

Instead of avoiding the theme of revenge, the Dardennes consciously play up ambiguous resemblances to revenge-driven films. The constant threat of bloodshed is evoked through the setting in the carpentry shop, where the ever-present power tools, chisels, knives, ropes, and heavy boards play on the stylistics of bloodshed. Roger Ebert has captured the play on horror in his review, in which he shares a certain amount of self-irritation:

> [Olivier] corrects a boy using a power saw. We wonder, because we have been beaten down by formula films, if someone is going to lose a finger or a hand. No. . . . Then he tells the woman he will take the boy after all. She says the boy is in the shower room. The handheld camera, which follows Olivier everywhere, usually in close medium shot, follows him as he looks around a corner (we intuit it is a corner; two walls form an apparent join). Is he watching the boy take a shower? Is Olivier gay? No. We have seen too many movies. (Ebert 2003)

One could in effect pitch a very different film from the same narrative material, one in which the main character plots to exact revenge by taking a job where he imagines his son's murderer will eventually pass; secretly he waits for a moment to strike. Jean-Pierre has implied as much: "Why did he decide to teach in that kind of school—a school where he is likely to meet someone like Francis? If he chose to teach there it is because one day he said to himself, perhaps unconsciously, that he was going to meet his son's murderer" (Dardenne 2003, 17).

In his *Pervert's Guide to Cinema*, Slavoj Žižek interprets the crime and horror cinema of directors such as Hitchcock and David Lynch as a visual depiction of the netherworld of subconscious drives. Visiting the bathroom in which the final scene of Coppola's *Conversation* (1974) was filmed, Žižek (2006) draws an analogy between the toilet and the cinema. At the end of the film, Gene Hackman searches the bathroom for clues to the murder he believes he has just witnessed; when he flushes the toilet, blood and gore begin to ooze up, pierce through to pollute a sterile environment. For Žižek, sitting in front of the film screen is analogous to sitting in front of a toilet bowl, staring at a "dark hole," waiting for the excrement of our psychological nether regions to come gushing out.

But, unsurprisingly in the Dardennes' very un-Lacanian and anti-psychological filmmaking, something very different is happening in *The Son*. Žižek declares his admiration for the scene in *Psycho* (1960) in which Norman Bates cleans up the bathroom after the murder of Marion Crane, which he interprets as a touching testimonial to the role of human labor to efface violent impulses. Work for Žižek is about "cleaning the traces of a stain," a stain that would betray the presence of some unknowable but violent Lacanian Real. In *The Son*, work operates as an agent of the law more effectively than Norman does in mopping up the outbreak of violent desires. The film is a visual poem to work and its teaching. Olivier measures with a glance whether something has been done right, is square or if it is out of proportion or balance. He recognizes when an apprentice has made a bad mortise, or when a spacing piece has not been cut on a miter box. There is something abstracting in his gaze, as if he holds a mental blueprint up to every piece of wood. He shows them how to hold their bodies as they saw, how to pick up beams and balance them on their shoulders, how to read blueprints. He addresses his apprentices by their first names, as the adults that they must become—though much of the communication is limited to directions on how to handle a tool or take a measurement.

Educating gives Olivier a semblance of balance in relation to his loss. Unlike most films on the subject of a dead child, *The Son* never uses montage to give flashbacks about Olivier's dead child, nor do we see photos or souvenirs of the boy in his apartment. We cannot relate in the slightest to the particularities of his loss, and we are confronted instead with the purely present and exterior expressions of a lonely man. Work gives him a way of occupying his solitude. In one touching scene, Olivier arrives home alone in his apartment to find a long series of messages on his answering machine. The austere and conspicuously bare apartment becomes populated with these voices from the exterior, one asking to sleep at his house for the night, another whether he would warn the caller's new employer of his fear of heights, another that the manual he has written is ready to be picked up from the copy service, yet another telling him that the caller has quit his job to work for his mother (an unstable alcoholic) in her café-bar. The emptiness of the apartment does not recede, but it is counterbalanced by the voices from outside, in a completely diegetic and secularized version of the portrait scene in *Falsch*.

There is a remarkable coherence between these themes of measurement and balance and the evolution of the Dardennes' camera use, which has for this film evolved to a point of utter precision. Again with Benoît Dervaux and Amaury Duquenne, the brothers mastered a new machine, the Aaton A-minima 16mm, whose light weight gave them an expanded range of possible movements and access (the camera is popular for shooting sporting events). The complex use of the camera can be illustrated by the opening scene. As in past films, the shots unfold from Olivier Gourmet's body. Toward the end of production, the opening scene was reshot so that the credits could roll over an extreme close-up of Gourmet's shoulder, which looks more like a dark shimmer of fabric than an identifiable body part. The camera moves up the fabric of his overalls, finally arriving at the back of Gourmet's head and neck. After a brief pivot, it moves back down his shoulder and arm toward Francis's dossier in his hand. The operator does not pan over Gourmet from a fixed position; the flexible viewfinder allows him instead to lift and lower the camera in a human-controlled tracking shot that travels the length of Gourmet's body.

The camera is positioned just as closely, if not more so, than in *Rosetta;* but it also pivots and refocuses in ways that measure the precise distances between Olivier and others. Jean-Pierre has explained that the brothers have, since *Rosetta,* exclusively used a medium-angle lens that nearly replicates the natural focus of the human eye, with a slight tightness that slightly sharpens the view of individual objects (Limousin 2006). In *Rosetta* background characters faded from sight. In *The Son* there are several important instances in which the image is refocused on a second character. Again at the start of the film, the camera pivots from the back of Olivier's head to Catherine's face. A brief adjustment brings her into focus; another adjustment brings Olivier back into focus when the camera points back toward him. The technique, used throughout the film, uses the camera to establish not just one character, but the distance between characters. In another memorable moment, Olivier sends Francis across the workshop to fetch a tool; the camera remains fixed on Olivier's face, but as we watch his intense eyes panning and refocusing on the boy, we have a precise idea of where Francis is, even off camera.

Both Olivier's equilibrium and the equilibrium of the camera are thrown off by Francis's arrival. Even in Olivier's home, when his ex-wife Magali visits to tell him that she is putting her life back together (she is remarrying and pregnant), the focus shifts repeatedly from Olivier's face to hers standing behind him, unable to focus on both in the same image, as if to underline the emotional gulf between them. Typically self-controlled, Olivier sneaks into the locker room alone and climbs a row of lockers to peer out of a high window at the new boy. When he hears a noise, he clambers down and sticks his nose quickly into his own locker. He begins to act weirdly, goes to the welding shop to see the boy, sneaks up to Catherine's office door. In the scene in front of her door we see how his jerky movements destabilize even the precision of the camera. The operator follows him closely until he stops, points the camera over his shoulder, and refocuses on Catherine inside the office and then on the boy's hand. The refocus measures distance, but we are frustrated by not seeing the boy, and when Francis stands up, Olivier is so startled that he races down the hall, nearly bumping into the camera.

The film also owes much to the work of the two actors, especially Olivier Gourmet, who took the best actor award at Cannes, but in a quieter way, Morgan Marinne as well. The Dardennes have stated that *The Son,* their third collaboration with Gourmet, was conceived in order to make a film around him, and they confess to "dreaming up imaginary situations" for him to play ever since the filming of *La promesse* (L. Dardenne 2008, 93). (For a portrait of Gourmet, see Avon 2002.) The result for *The Son* is what Sotinel has called the "osmosis between the film and the character," or perhaps between the film and the actor's relation to others might be a better way of putting it (Sotinel 2002). For *The Son* reflects the Dardennes' desire to make a film "without a subject," one that would concentrate only on bodies and their relations and positions with respect to each other. Even relations on the set reflected the tension between Olivier and Francis. In one interview Gourmet speaks of the difference between the set of *La promesse* and that of *The Son* (in a bonus feature on *The Son*). With Jérémie Renier (Igor) Gourmet had made an effort to become close friends with Renier and invited him to his home and out for drinks months before filming began. Marinne, by the Dardennes' account, was chosen to play Francis in part because he conveyed a sense of fragility and hidden secrets. On the set Gourmet sensed his vulnerability and need for moral support but, with the Dardennes' agreement, created an apprehensive atmosphere by avoiding Marinne and speaking to him only when absolutely necessary.

It is to maintain a dreadful sense of indecision that *The Son* unfolds in an increasingly terse spiral of potentially violent encounters, using a looming musical repetition and intensification rather than narrative linearity. The brothers use the motifs of hands, work, and touch to create rhythm and tension. Olivier teaches by touching, by sawing, feeling, weighing, running his fingers over surfaces. When a boy starts to bang a piece of wood into a joint with a lead hammer, Olivier deftly grabs it and replaces it with a wooden mallet. But with Francis's arrival, Olivier's hands become agitated. He looks for activities to distract them: drinking coffee from his thermos, drying his lunch plate, washing in the sink, and so on. A number of scenes show Olivier stiffening up to avoid contact when Francis comes near him. We see this when he teaches the group how to mount a ladder with heavy beams on their shoulders. He shows them how to bend to pick up the wood and balance the beam on a shoulder and describes to them how to stay close to the ladder as he mounts the rungs. When his turn comes, Francis begins to lose balance. Though Olivier barks out directions to him and climbs up behind him to grab the beam, Francis panics, sitting down squarely on Olivier's neck—boy, board, and teacher fall. Angry over the imposed contact, Olivier screams at the boy while rubbing his neck.

But this touch is not only threatening. After falling, Francis sits on the floor, holding his head between his knees, hands behind his head, in an almost fetal position. Olivier seems moved by the boy's need and makes him repeat the move until he gets things right. The boy is a perfect illustration of the need for rehabilitation centers: sleepy, overmedicated, Francis is somewhat disconnected, but respectful, friendly with the other boys, and open to learning carpentry. Even in the first encounter with the boy, the one described by Ebert, Olivier's built-up rage finds Francis sleeping like an infant in the welding room lockers. Francis has no family to speak of, his mother's boyfriend won't let her see him, and he has no idea where his father is. He is uneducated enough that he doesn't understand Olivier when he tells him to write his initials on his folding ruler. Olivier is not blind with rage, for he can precisely measure Francis's need, just as he can measure the size of overalls the boy needs with a single glance.

This knowledge only adds to Olivier's angst, as in an oft-discussed scene in which Olivier and Francis meet by chance at a sausage-and-fries take-out restaurant. Leaving with a sandwich in hand, someone brushes by Olivier, and we hear a voice speak—"you are hungry too sir"—and the camera quickly swings to reveal Francis, whose apparition has spooked Olivier. Reluctantly, but impelled by none but himself, Olivier chomps on his sandwich while leaning on his car, waiting for Francis to join him. Francis expresses admiration for Olivier's canny ability to measure with his eyes. Olivier responds that it is a matter of habit, a learned skill. Francis tests him by asking the distance between a paving stone and a car, and then between his own left foot and Olivier's right foot. He hands Olivier his bag of fries and takes out his folding ruler, which he carries with him even outside the classroom, perhaps in imitation of Olivier. Olivier is able to guess the distances to the centimeter. The moment has the potential to bond the two; but Olivier puts an end to it, gets in his car, and drives away.

As in *Rosetta,* the Dardennes often set Olivier in the place of the other. In one scene, he steals the key to Francis's apartment and stops by to snoop around. For once, the camera does not follow Olivier around the room but waits in a corner, observing him from a distance. The scene is back-lit by a window with a thin pink curtain, so that Olivier's face is not clear. He peers out the window, sits down at the table, gets up, approaches the bed, and lies down, scanning the room. Too big for the bed, he must twist himself in and lift his heavy boots onto the mattress; and, since the camera does not reposition itself (it seems to have been waiting for this shot), he is extremely foreshortened (figure 15). On one hand, he could be staking out a murder. At the same time, Olivier may be trying to literally put himself in Francis's place. The characters' empty home environments resemble each other. Like Olivier's, the boy's apartment contains almost nothing: a bottle of milk, an ashtray, a dirty glass on the table, a radio, some medication, and an alarm clock next to an unmade bed. What is he doing here? He doesn't know (the phrase "I don't know" is repeated several times by Olivier throughout the film), and because of the strange distance between him and the camera, because of the lighting, and because of the angles, neither do we.

This scene, Olivier's devotion to his students, and the images of Olivier teaching Francis suggest that the horror-genre ambiguities of the

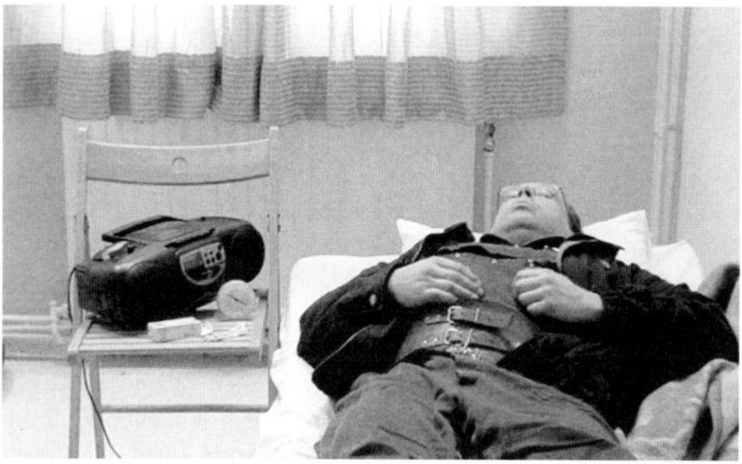

Figure 15. Olivier in Francis's apartment.

film should not be overemphasized (we *have* seen too many movies). Olivier is not devoured by a need to kill his son's killer. Perhaps his attraction to Francis stems from an attempt to understand what happened, to hear Francis admit to the crime, and perhaps to hear him proclaim his guilt and remorse. Olivier is an orderly man who cannot get a handle on the past, though Francis provides a link to it. Nonetheless, what he precisely wants seems unclear, hence his repetition of the expression "I don't know." Ideas of revenge seem to rise to the surface only at moments of major frustration, when Olivier's attempts to come to terms with his son's death are thwarted by Francis's unresponsiveness.

The tense moments increase in duration throughout the film, building in a crescendo. At the beginning there are dreaded moments of possible contact, then an increasing series of short interactions as the two work together, until finally almost interminable sequence shots, lasting several minutes, in which the various "instruments" in the Dardennes' orchestral work struggle to find rhythm or harmony. The tension reaches its highest pitch during a long scene, on a Saturday morning, when Olivier invites Francis to visit a remote lumberyard to teach him how to identify wood. They arrive at the school early, hitch a trailer to Olivier's car, pick up a tarp and some rope, and head off into the country. This sequence fills most of the last third of the film.

The automobile scene, long a test of directors' creativity, is filmed in a way that intensifies the ambiguities of the film. The automobile itself has been a preferred location of theirs since *Il court il court le monde* and *Thinking of You* and has also been the object of renewed creative explorations by other directors such as Jim Jarmusch's *Night on Earth* (1991), Abbas Kiarostami's *Taste of Cherry* (1997) and *Ten* (2002), or Claire Denis's *Vendredi soir* (2002). *The Son* bears resemblances to each of these films, but perhaps most to Kiarostami's *Ten*. For the Dardennes, as for Kiarostami, who likens the automobile to a "room of a few cubic feet," the automobile offers a claustrophobic space. In this restricted space, especially in the very long sequence shots in which they are presented, passions grow stronger and more dangerous. The scene begins silently, but in the silence we become attuned to the sounds of the car. The smallest movements of the actors take on great importance. Even the car itself becomes another potential weapon. At one point the overmedicated boy naturally falls asleep, though Olivier takes it as an insult.

The man's eyes begin to dart back and forth, from the sleeping boy to the rearview mirror and then to the road. Suddenly he slams on the brakes and the boy flies onto the dash—the camera is also bounced around.

The setup of the scene is complex and suggestive. Instead of fixing digital video cameras on the car's dashboard (Kiarostami's almost impersonal method), the Dardennes film, from the backseat, the back of Olivier's and Francis's heads, making the space beyond the windshield move erratically and out of focus, drawing all our attention to the inside of the car. At the beginning of the sequence, the operator is in the backseat, filming the characters as they speak, and then, for a long moment, aiming at Olivier after Francis has fallen asleep. After he is awoken by Olivier, Francis asks whether he can climb in back to continue sleeping. As he moves between the two front seats into the back, the camera operator must squeeze out of the way (again exploiting the lightweight camera) while pointing the camera at a toolbox on the backseat floor. (Jean-Pierre Dardenne explained to me that at this point Gourmet pressed a rigged switch to send the passenger's seat far forward, giving the cameraman room to film the boy stretching out in back before panning up to frame Olivier.) The trick allows the brothers to reveal, in one continuous shot, practically the entire interior of the car without a trace of the machinery, demonstrating as much as any other shot their "desire to be inside of things" (L. Dardenne 2008, 138). In contrast to the camera handling in Kiarostami, in *The Son* the operator, or some human presence, *is* there in the tension even if unseen, unheard, and detached from the actors' faces.

This human presence is hauntingly suggestive of how we view Olivier throughout the film. After showing the film to an audience in Japan, the Dardennes fielded a comment from a man whose son had been murdered, and who had become an opponent of the death penalty. The man shared a Japanese saying with the brothers: "a child grows up seeing his father's back" (L. Dardenne 2008, 154). Indeed, throughout the film the camera has often borrowed this perspective, showing closely the nape of Olivier's neck. After watching it so long and in such continuity, we have grown as familiar with it, with the cut of his hair and the mole on his right ear, as we do with family members or friends, like children ourselves. Watching Olivier and Francis in the front seat may even be reminiscent of family car trips, with one child in the back watching his family conversing up front. We switch places with our brother when he is tired, looking at him and the father with concern in this tense moment. Like Olivier in Francis's room, we take the place of another, and there are many strange resemblances between the mute presence of Olivier's son and our own perspective in this film. We watch as if ghosts ourselves, move silently out of the way of moving bodies, observing Olivier when he interacts with the boy or when, thinking he is alone, behaves with pettiness. And Francis, spread out across the back seat, takes our place, even literally resembles the position and limpness of Olivier's son after being strangled, creating even closer analogies between ourselves, the dead son, and the killer, though without a hint of identification.

The automobile sequence, with Olivier and this unsuspecting victim traveling alone to a remote location, also gives the Dardennes a chance to update another figuration of the father–son relationship that has interested them over the years: the story of Abraham and Isaac. For it is as if the camera were taking the place of Johannes de Silentio, in Søren Kierkegaard's canonical treatment of the story in *Fear and Trembling*, whose "craving was to go along on the three-day journey when Abraham rode with sorrow before him and Isaac beside him" (Kierkegaard 1983, 9). The thick atmosphere of these long *plans séquence* force the viewer to live through the emotional experience that such a three-day journey would entail (the film was originally called *L'Épreuve*, or "the test" or "ordeal"—words that appear throughout *Fear and Trembling*).

The telling of Abraham and Isaac's story reveals much about the Dardennes' treatment of the cultural inheritance of growing up in Catholic Belgium. Though the Dardennes themselves have declined to endorse any position on religion, Luc's journal does refer on numerous occasions to a search for meaning after the "death of god." Writing specifically about Abraham and Isaac, he wonders: "how can we inherit meaning from our childhood Bible readings when God can no longer be found?" (L. Dardenne 2008, 19). Secularizing this particular story is all the more difficult, since Abraham's sacrifice of Isaac has often been interpreted, as it is by Kierkegaard, as a parable of faith itself. Abraham willingly accepts the killing of his son only because he has faith in the voice of God who tells him to do so. Kierkegaard's narrator, Johannes de Silentio, is endlessly astounded by Abraham's behavior, which is completely incomprehensible according to the language of ethics. Indeed, Kierkegaard argues, from an ethical perspective, "what Abraham did was that he meant to murder Isaac" (Kierkegaard 1983, 30). Ethics would require that Abraham stop "at every station along the way," turn around, and tell God that if he wanted Isaac he would have to take him Himself (32). But he has made a "leap of faith," out of the ethical realm to an individual and direct relation to God. His intention to kill his son, never in doubt, is transformed through faith from murder into sacrifice (30) (figure 16).

The Son is an exploration of how to keep ethics from spiraling into sacrifice. The difference between Kierkegaard's Abraham and the Dardennes' Olivier becomes clear if we consider how each of them speaks. On the road, Isaac innocently asks his father where he has hidden away the sacrificial lamb. Abraham can only repeat: "God will provide the lamb for the sacrifice." He falls silent (a silence held in awe by Johannes de Silentio). For Kierkegaard, this is a direct result of his leap of faith; Abraham cannot explain, simply because there are no words to communicate an action founded entirely on his belief that God will fix things. Olivier also keeps silent about the most important secret, his true relation to Francis and his deep anger. But this has nothing to do with faith. Luc has written of "Abraham's hope that the murder will not happen, that God will provide. In Olivier's silence there is the rising tide of his

Figure 16. Olivier/Abraham prepares for the sacrifice.

intent to kill" (L. Dardenne 2008, 137). In the religious context, God rewards Abraham for his obedience by safeguarding his son. Without a god there is no guarantee; there is simply the danger of conspirators committing murder (L. Dardenne 2008, 19).

But against the dread-filled hum of the engine and changing gears, the words of the characters develop into a tentative discussion. Olivier and Francis find themselves engaged in a type of Levinasian conversation, bringing them toward one another and making them confront their responsibilities. For Olivier, this means constantly responding to Francis's filial addresses: first by teaching him about the rings in tree trunks and the qualities of different woods. Francis even asks Olivier, during a stop for lunch, to be his legal guardian, or *tuteur.* But conversation leads in both directions, and Francis must return over and again to his crime as Olivier asks him about his family and his time at Fraipont. Jean-Pierre has explained that the film is in great part "about the difficulty of speaking: Olivier has difficulty saying, 'It was my son you killed,' and Francis has difficulty saying what he had done" (Dardenne 2003, 19). In the car they pursue the most tenuous conversation, "impossible words" according to Luc, but words that, as in *La promesse,* put the characters on the ethical or educational level: These conversations are their "last attempt to find each other, to find again the human being that they could be, that they were, and which they can no longer remember, but which their words still believe in" (L. Dardenne 2008, 115). Olivier presses him on the crime over a game of foosball, claiming that as his *tuteur* he has the right to ask such questions. But back in the car the conversation does not completely come together—all Olivier can get out of the drowsy Francis is that there was "other stuff" besides the robbery. Olivier is so angry that he overshoots the entrance of the lumberyard. The automobile sequence ends in a stalemate when they arrive at the lumberyard and Francis admits to regretting the crime only because he had to spend five years in detention; he blithely adds that he has to have a piss before hopping out of the car.

Olivier and Francis pick up their exchange once they have entered the warehouse. Though Olivier seethes at Francis, their words become even more firmly entwined. Everyday dialogue about topics as banal as types of wood has rarely if ever been so precious in the cinema as when the two walk through the warehouse side by side: "Why are there pieces of wood between the boards on the pallets?" asks Francis. "So they can dry," he replies, but his answer draws him in deeper: "if you build a door with wood that hasn't dried . . ." Francis finishes his thought: "it shrinks." Olivier continues, "Right, and you'll have spaces between the planks." Dialogue builds a discursive bond almost against Olivier's wishes. It erodes his anger to see that Francis has been studying his manual. The two also continue to work together, if tensely. Olivier lowers planks from a stack of pallets down to Francis and they carry them together to cut on a saw. By carrying the long planks together, each with one end on his shoulders, their strides come naturally together in rhythm (figure 17).

The conclusion of the film begins in a saw room where the two cut the long planks down to fit into the trailer. As he helps Francis measure, Olivier asks a quick calculation—divide 5 meters 80 by two—to which Francis answers without hesitation. The camera pans back and forth between their faces, again taking its movement cue from the distance between them. As they work together, Olivier rather unclimactically blurts out his secret (we hear it off screen as the camera passes between them), almost as if he were blurting out a phrase without knowing what the consequences will be: "the boy you killed was my child." The surprised camera jumps quickly to Olivier and then Francis, linking them in their reaction to these words. Francis, now thinking he knows why

Figure 17. Working together. |

he has been brought here, immediately runs out of the room, Olivier chasing him. The wood in the lumberyard no longer connects them but becomes obstacles that Francis throws between him and Olivier in self-defense. In contrast to the car, the warehouse is filled with stacks upon stacks of drying wood and provides many crannies to hide in. The objects display their two faces, oscillating between a narrative of education and a narrative of revenge.

The last two long sequence shots take place outdoors, where Francis has hoped to escape into the woods. The natural setting is filmed in a lovely twilight among the pine trees, a setting found also in *Rosetta* and in the Dardennes' latest film, *The Silence of Lorna* (2008). If in the documentaries the appearance of nature was limited to the vegetation-covered slagheaps around Liège, it here represents an escape from the enclosed settings of most of the film. For Luc Dardenne, the forest has something "maternal" to it, at least in this film, where it nurtures the ethical event that is about to take place (Dardenne 2008). There is also perhaps a symbolic connection between these trees and the pine that has been the subject of Olivier's attempts at teaching, linking education to a natural state of things.

The sequence opens with the spark of violence that we have half feared, half expected, throughout the film. Olivier tackles the boy, and after a struggle, pins him down with his knees on the youth's chest. He wraps his hands around Francis's throat and, for a long moment, squeezes (the camera remains fixed on Olivier's face, more intrigued by his decision than by the scandalous and dreadful crime). There is a harrowing face-to-face moment as the two stare into each other's eyes. But Olivier's breathing finally becomes heavy and he releases his grip. He rolls off the boy and they sit next to each other. The man starts to weep uncontrollably, almost blubbering for several moments, before walking away bitterly, the camera remaining behind as he disappears. It is a common reaction to this scene to conclude that Olivier has forgiven Francis. *Cahiers* critic Jean-Sébastian Chauvin, for example, at the end of an otherwise insightful review, criticized this and the next scene for a lack of realism: "A question still remains: a man can forgive the killer of his son, but can he accept to teach him and work by his side, as the last shot suggests?" (Chauvin 2002, 81). However, as Jean-Pierre states it, "these actions might be understood as a kind of forgiveness by some people; but Olivier does not say, "I forgive you" to the boy, and the boy does not say, "I ask your pardon" (Dardenne 2003, 19). As his bitter tears and his walking away suggest, Olivier has not lost the hurt or washed away Francis's guilt, but he has lost his desire for violence.

In fact, the clarity with which we see Francis's eyes in this penultimate scene, and the lingering camera, suggest a change in emphasis in the *mise-en-scène* from Olivier to Francis. This shift is reinforced in the last *plan séquence,* which brings us back to the car, where Olivier is arranging the wood planks on his trailer. He looks momentarily surprised and a pan brings us to Francis, shown from head to toe and alone in the shot for the first time. It is now time for the boy to act, to continue the face-to-face encounter; even despite Olivier's hard glare, he approaches, cringingly picks up the last board, and places it on the trailer. Francis hasn't spoken a word since the warehouse, but his silent action now expresses a consciousness. In a film about their work made by Jean-Pierre Limousin, the Dardennes refer to another biblical story that they rework to an ethical outcome: Cain and Abel. When God asks Cain "Where is your brother?" Cain replies, "How am I to know; am I my brother's keeper?" The Dardennes interpret what usually is seen as evasiveness as a sign of a moral awakening. For Cain to speak in this way, he must be conscious of his guilt. Like Rosetta, Francis has realized that he is a part of a relation, through law and guilt, and he has learned this from Olivier. He can now get to work. On the other hand, Olivier does not have the power to choose, to teach or not to teach, to forgive or not to forgive, to be a father to Francis or not; he is already in some sense Francis's father, since he has planted the seeds of an ethical consciousness. The unrelenting insistence on the back of characters' heads throughout the film pays off here, even if it tries the patience of some viewers: Francis and Olivier are not personalities or psychologies, but people who begin to emerge from their instincts—moral lethargy or uncontrolled vengeance—as autonomous ethical beings as they finally face each other.

The battling musical themes of the film do not find a happy resolution at the end, but their discord does manage a modicum of calm. There is even some hint that this experience might help Olivier step out from the shadow of his son. After the wood has been loaded into the trailer, the two wrap plastic tarp around the boards, using the rope that was meant for killing. As Olivier folds the tarp under the boards, they take on an eerie resemblance to a shrouded body (while playing Roger in *La promesse,* Gourmet had used a very similar tarp to wrap up Hamidou's body before hiding it under a door) (figure 18). Weapons become plowshares; and the wood itself, the object of education in this film, becomes sacred, the sacrificial lamb that absorbs the violence to heal the group's wounds. But there is a difference between law and sacrifice. By accepting calm without complete harmony, the Dardennes do not require a victim, whether it is Francis, killed for the memory of the dead child, or even a biblical messiah supposed to suffer for us all. It requires a project and a moral law, the civilizing process of teaching and work. The dead are in a moving but secular sense buried, though not erased, and Olivier can recommence his life. Another potential title for the film was in fact *Vivre,* and Luc praises in his diary the ending of Nanni Moretti's film *The Son's Room* (2001), in which life seems to return slowly to the grieving family. The film is perhaps as powerful a commentary on the tragedy of double-digit unemployment as was *Rosetta.*

The Son deals critically with issues much broader that it might seem at first viewing, and as often happens, the recurrence of a theme can indicate a deeper cultural malaise. A final context in which to read this rich film is the political moment at which it was released, a moment at which

Figure 18. Burying the dead. |

recrimination and vengeance were in the daily news and other media around the globe. *Cahiers* editor Charles Tesson reads the father figures of several films from 2002 as indirect attempts to deal with the terrorist attacks a year earlier (Tesson 2002, 5). The period was of course marked by the aftermath of 9-11, the war in Afghanistan, the Bush doctrine, and the build-up of the case to invade Iraq. These issues may indeed explain in part why fatherhood and many of its associated themes—paternal authority, impotence, revenge, violence, and the law—found their way into Spielberg's *Minority Report*, and also M. Night Shyamalan's *Signs*, both released at about the same time as *The Son*. The Dardennes' own reaction to the 9-11 attacks on the Twin Towers was shock at public intellectuals who seemed to take pleasure in seeing the fall of Empire, or who expressed admiration for the "beauty" of the terrorist act. And yet their secular parable of a father who refuses to take advantage of his power to kill was inconsistent with the atmosphere of recrimination that seeped into the movies; embracing the law, the film was out of harmony with a time out of joint. We have indeed seen too many movies.

The Rhythm of Tears: *The Child*

Many of the Dardennes' films include moments of intense emotion in which a character, and often the audience with the character, is physically overwhelmed by tears. Igor cries tears of frustration as his attraction to Assita brings him further from his father; Rosetta sheds tears of exhaustion and bewilderment as she turns to Riquet; Olivier is cleansed by tears of mourning at the end of *The Son*. In each of these cases, tears are solitary, shed by one person alone, even if they involve, indirectly, a relation to another. The Dardennes' next film, *The Child* (2005), picks up the thread of tears, this time to explore the circumstances under which they are shed, but most important, shared. The film deals more directly with affect, but also with love and reconciliation into a bond sealed by tears.

The narrative encompasses a few days in the life of Bruno, played again by Jérémie Renier, the ringleader of a group of child thieves. At the beginning of the film, Bruno's girlfriend, Sonia, returns to the streets from giving birth to their child, Jimmy. Selfish, unattached, narcissistic, and completely devoid of a sense of responsibility, Bruno sells the child, after shockingly little hesitation, to an illegal adoption ring, earning five thousand euros in the deal. Upon learning what he has done, Sonia faints, must be taken to the hospital, and denounces Bruno to the police. Bruno frantically retrieves the baby, but falls in debt to a dangerous Mafioso to whom he had made the sale, becoming embroiled in two narratives: one melodramatic, involving his betrayal of Sonia; the other criminal, in which he must deal with an increasingly menacing mob of gangsters. After a failed purse snatching that proves nearly fatal to his accomplice (while the two hide in the Meuse, the boy becomes paralyzed from the cold), Bruno seems to undergo a hidden but major transformation. He surrenders himself to the police so that the boy does not take the blame for the crime. The very last scene of the film is arguably the most important. Sonia comes to visit Bruno in the prison; they begin to speak, but instead cry until the screen goes dark.

The Child bears, as Louis Héliot has noted, a resemblance to the melodrama of Frank Capra's *It's a Wonderful Life* (1947) or Douglas Sirk's *Imitation of Life* (1959) (Héliot 2005, 138). The resemblance, however, is not evident at first glance, since nothing seems more antithetical to the Dardennes than some of the soppy trappings of such films: elaborate sets and costumes, famous actors, running makeup, and overwrought dialogue. Doubtlessly more important than the genre per se is a single melodramatic forebear, Murnau's *Sunrise*, subtitled "a song of two humans." Often mentioned in the Dardennes' interviews and writings, *Sunrise* tells the story of a young peasant who is tempted by a "woman from the city" to drown his wife. At the last moment, in the boat as he prepares to kill her, he has a change of heart; instead he brings his wife to the city and spends the night trying to regain her trust and love. *The Child* tells a very different story and does not have the expressionist qualities of Murnau's sets. *Sunrise* is rather, for the Dardennes, a matter of rhythm: The couple does not come together immediately, but slowly through the night while they spend time getting their hair cut, eating and dancing at a nice restaurant, visiting a carnival, and participating in other amusements of the city. Murnau's film comprises a series of actions often shot in very long takes, linked together by the rhythmic editing common to the tradition of the integrity of the shot. (See Magny 2005 for an extended analysis.)

Every Dardenne film, since the frenetic early documentaries, unfolds through a rhythmic editing. In *La promesse,* long *plans séquence* lure the viewer into the temporal development of the shot, and abrupt cuts move the viewer into a new time, a new rhythmic stage. *Rosetta* was a stormy pursuit to complete exhaustion, punctuated by moments of fragile calm. *The Son* was tension-ridden, with two ominous lines playing against each other against a background of muted but menacing ambient sounds. *The Child* also unfolds as a series of temporal units. But it follows a more varied rhythm filled with alternation and counterpoint, stops and pauses, scenes of great *allégresse,* dancelike scenes, and one floating, harmonious scene to end the film.

The rhythm of *The Child* is often halting or alternating. The inspiration for the film was itself a case of noticing an absence. According to the brothers, they had once seen a young mother violently pushing a buggy through Seraing, "as if she were fleeing from it" (L. Dardenne 2008, 134). Thinking of this scene, they eventually became interested in an absent player, the father. This absence could be seen as the melodic principle guiding the film. The first scene opens with an image of Sonia climbing the stairs to her apartment with her newborn baby in her arms. But our attention shifts immediately to Bruno, through his absence from the frame, for he has sublet her apartment for the week she spent giving birth and the shady-looking tenants slam the door in her face. The next scenes again follow Sonia, but their focus is again Bruno's absence as she tries to call him and then hitches a moped ride to look for him. She finally finds him panhandling coins from cars in traffic while watching a man in a bar and they are at last framed in one shot. And yet Bruno is distracted, as if he does not much like this family portrait, thinking more about the man his gang wants to mug. Throughout the film the couple is rarely together, giving the film an alternating organization, "one shot for him, one for her" (Bégaudaud 2005, 25). A halting, disjointed rhythm results from these two lines of melody that cannot appear in the same measure.

According to one social worker, Seraing is an almost hopelessly marginalized society: "in the Molinay quarter, most children have never seen their parents work" (M.S. 2005). But instead of depressed, the atmosphere of *The Child* is carnivalesque and irresponsible, as the lack of future has led almost everyone to a life of petty crime. Bruno has been called "Faginlike" by many commentators because he is the head of the gang, but in many ways he more resembles the child thieves of Dickens's *Oliver Twist,* as does his accomplice Steve (Jérémie Ségard), a prematurely aged little bandit and hard bargainer in the mold of the Artful Dodger. There is a carefree nihilism in these characters. Everyone zips around town on mopeds, without helmets, even carrying the newborn on their lap. (Speed functions a bit like in *Il court il court le monde,* as a rather pathetic distraction from real life.) Bruno is the most extreme example. Work, he says, is for *cons,* or "asses," and he prefers his life without attachments. Bruno cares more about his leather jacket and its racing stripes down the sleeves than about where he will spend the night (usually in a homeless shelter or in his hideout on the banks of the Meuse). In his childish way Bruno even turns boredom into play, stomping in mud and karate kicking a wall to see how high he can leave a print, or splashing in the water of the Meuse with a metal rod (perhaps with a hint of Narcissus staring at his image in the water). His criminal activities flow fluidly from one to the next; in one telling example, Bruno, after being thrown out by Sonia for selling the kid, pawns Jimmy's stroller in a secondhand store, bargains relentlessly for the best price—not forgetting to sell Sonia's sweater, accidentally left in the buggy, for a euro—all while staking out a purse snatching from the store's proprietor.

Within the confines of his fictional world, Bruno, with his leather jacket and noiresque hat gives the impression of a hustler on the move. But the Dardennes counteract his self-image with their framing. Bruno is not so difficult to follow as Rosetta, and we are not measuring the distance between him and another as in *The Son.* The image is more balanced, the camera steadier and at times positioned further away, providing a larger and more stable setting. And yet, in full shot, mid-shot, or even mid-close-up, Bruno is most often alone, against one of the brick walls that have become omnipresent in the Dardennes' work, separated from the social life of the city. The wider perspective makes shots more static, producing an excruciating slowness, as we watch Bruno take a bus, wait outside Sonia's door, stake out a robbery, or meet one of his fellow gang members. Throughout most of *The Child* one finds slightly less of Van der Keuken's empathy and slightly more of a Bressonian detachment.

The audience quickly forms a moral judgment of Bruno and then moves on, or as Manohla Dargis writes in her review, "since there is no moral ambiguity in the act of selling another human being, there would be no point in such judgment, other than to indulge in some self-satisfied finger-wagging" (Dargis 2006). At times we even glimpse some redeeming affect in Bruno, especially in his relationship with Sonia. We see this in a lovely scene in which Bruno and Sonia are together, momentarily breaking the alternation of single-character shots. Bruno squanders all the money he acquires in a robbery to rent a convertible for the day and buy a buggy for Jimmy, whom they put in the backseat of the car. On the road, Bruno and Sonia bicker affectionately over radio selections. Sonia puts on a pleasant waltz that calms Jimmy; Bruno wants something more rock. While wrestling over the dials, Sonia puts Bruno's hand into her teeth and swings playfully in time with the music. Once they stop in a park, the two chase each other around the car and lovingly lean their foreheads together, giggling and kissing with sandwiches in their hands (figure 19). Sonia shakes up a soft drink and opens it, sending soda all over Bruno, who tackles her in the grass, in amorous play that is not free of childishness: Thomas Sotinel calls it a "bagarre de cour de recréation" or "recess-period roughhousing" (Sotinel 2005). The automobile scene stands out because the characters are together, but also because of its flowing rhythm, guided by the beat of the waltz, a dancelike counterpoint to the excruciating plodding of Bruno alone.

Figure 19. Young lovers embrace.

We do not, however, forget the irresponsibility that surrounds this action. The camera does not follow Sonia and Bruno but remains with the car watching them run off, as if the presence of the baby were keeping us from being involved in their happiness. The film often emphasizes a kind of "elephant in the room" effect of the unseen or the off-screen in this way. When we watch Sonia, we sense that her irritation often comes from Bruno's absence. When we watch Bruno behaving stupidly or irresponsibly, we judge his actions with Sonia in the back of our minds. More important, our judgment of both characters takes place with the baby in mind. As Sonia and Bruno fool around, we may be thinking that Sonia should not be running like that so soon after having a baby, or that they shouldn't be smoking, riding mopeds, or having sex. Our opinion of Sonia improves as she seems to accept the responsibilities and even joys of motherhood, whereas our opinion of Bruno does not. In both cases our opinion is colored by the presence of the baby, and yet, though it was played by seventeen newborns and one rubber imitation baby (all acknowledged in the credits), baby Jimmy is kept mainly off screen or hidden in his swaddling.

Indeed, throughout *The Child* there is a teeming off-screen space, one that has never been as elaborately developed in the Dardennes' oeuvre as it is here. It is particularly rich in scenes that touch upon the sale and repurchase of the baby, in which the Dardennes take advantage of the suggestiveness of sound. When entering the building to sell Jimmy, Bruno's cell phone rings, and he follows the directions into a lobby. To assuage a little guilt, he asks whether the baby's family will have a lot of money. A quick call from Sonia, to which he replies that he is in the park with Jimmy, reminds him and the viewer of the gravity of his action. The elevator is not working, so Bruno must take Jimmy out of the buggy—in one of the few shots where we actually see the baby. In one long sequence shot he carries him to a dark, empty room, dimly backlit through a thick red curtain. He takes off his jacket while holding the child, lays it on the floor, and places the child on it before exiting to an adjacent room. Another telephone call, and Bruno, following orders of the voice on the line, shuts the door between him and the boy. He stands against a wall with dingy patterned wallpaper, a dark portrait of him alone, but with rich hushed noises surrounding him—steps and the baby coughing in the next room. The frame remains on Bruno until the annoying phone rings again and he is told that he may reenter. He takes the money and his jacket and then leaves—the baby has disappeared into the obscure off-screen space, and money has appeared almost magically in the baby's place.

Later, after Sonia rants deliriously and dangerously about the baby at the hospital, Bruno panics and arranges to buy Jimmy back. Again everything happens off-screen. The exchange takes place at an abandoned storage garage, which is again exploited theatrically by the brothers. Bruno waits again in a dark, enclosed space, this time against a cinder-block wall. We hear a car arrive, a door slam, the shutters of the garage next door slide open, and a voice pronounce "the money." Bruno speaks nervously to the faceless voice as he searches for something to stand on to hand the money through a light-filled opening high in the wall. We hear the shuffling of bills while the camera returns to Bruno's face. The voice doesn't answer when Bruno asks whether the baby is there, and only demands a missing bill. Apologizing, Bruno says he inadvertently left it in his pocket. The voice tells him to wait for the sound of the car to disappear before coming out. Luckily the baby is left in a neighboring garage, and Bruno seems pleased that he could make Jimmy reappear in such an economical way.

But the off-screen encroaches increasingly on Bruno's onscreen world. Already the voice in the garage makes him nervous. Then the adoption ring makes itself visible when one of the Mafiosi (played by Fabrice Rongione) approaches Bruno and tells him to return to the garage the next day to work out a deal for paying back the organization the money it lost on the failed deal. When Bruno misses his appointment, the Mafia bursts into his solitude with brutality. Bruno is beaten savagely in a bar and alley, robbed of his last cent, and it is made clear to him that he is in debt and will remain so for many years. He crawls off to sleep in his bunker, wrapping himself in a cardboard box like a coffin. This narrative thread is not exactly suspenseful, but marked with sudden bursts of violent action. Here the film approaches the rhythm of a film that Luc discusses in *Au dos de nos images,* Howard Hawks's *Red River* (1948), in which life on a cattle drive led by Mathew Garth (Montgomery Clift) also varies from slowness to sudden bursts of speed, with the constant danger of violence represented by the revenge that Thomas Dunson (John Wayne) has promised to exact before they reach the city (L. Dardenne 2008, 147). The violence of Bruno's beating shows what the Dardennes could indeed achieve if ever they chose to shoot a genre film.

While the crime narrative hangs over Bruno's head, the Dardennes concentrate on his daily existence, where the tempo is also mixed, and just as physical and ultimately more powerful. We see Bruno slowly coming into literal contact with others in the frame, touching them, but more important, holding them and coming to terms with their weight. This begins with the baby holding tenderly onto his neck as Bruno maneuvers up the stairs and through some dark hallways to sell him. The scene is reminiscent of the one in *Falsch* in which Joseph carries Bela in his arms, the scene that helped the brothers discover the body of the actor. Igor experiences a similar weight when Sonia faints. As he talks, Sonia's brain doesn't register: she merely repeats the same question over and over—Where is Jimmy? Rather pleased with his plan to tell the police that he fell asleep in a park and that the baby was stolen, he holds a cigarette out to her lips. But Sonia's body does register; her lips refuse, and when she sees the money he made, she faints. The Dardennes avoid cliché in this potentially very melodramatic scene through the sheer massiveness of her fall. She tries once to get up and flee Bruno but falls again, while the camera circles around the couple conveying the confusion of the scene. Whenever Bruno carries someone, the Dardennes exploit the *plan séquence* to underline both duration and weight: barely larger than Deborah François, Jérémie Renier must carry her limp body up some twenty steps from the hideout without a cut. Like Rosetta with her propane bottle or her mother, Bruno carries things to the edge of his physical potential.

There are other scenes with the experience of weight as well, such as when Sonia attacks him with a knife and he must struggle to escape. But none of these scenes impresses gravity on Bruno so much as his and Steve's botched attempt at purse snatching. The sequence begins with one more acceleration in tempo, in a chase scene as the two zip along on Steve's moped through the streets of Seraing to elude some witnesses who chase them in a car. The scene was filmed from a specially modified moped designed with a seat on the back for the cameraman to remain close to the action. While attempting to pass a narrow opening near Bruno's hideout, one of the tires of the moped is punctured by a sharp wire. Seeing the men arrive, Bruno leads Steve into the Meuse, where they hide under a disused portion of what looks like a dock by holding onto a piece of metal sticking out of it. Fear and the cold of the water paralyze Steve; he loses his grip on the metal and drifts out into the river. The self-adoring Narcissus himself slips below the surface as Steve holds onto him. But Bruno is able to drag him to the bank and to the hideout, where he warms his legs. He then goes to retrieve the money, but the police arrive and take Steve away.

There is also an interesting contrast in the brothers' manner of filming the Meuse and another canonical film involving the filming of water, Jean Vigo's *L'Atalante* (1934), which tells the story of love on a barge that travels the canals of France. Gilles Deleuze has in fact deduced an entire genre of image out of the filming of water by Vigo and Jean Renoir (in *Boudu sauvé des eaux*, for example), which he calls the *reume* or "liquid-image" (Deleuze 1986, 76–80). Playing on the "displacement of the centre of gravity" that comes in the water, Deleuze associates the reume with a "different regime," with more "balance" of "perceptions, affections, and actions" among men from the sea as opposed to men on land. Such different perceptions of "the 'objectivity' of bodies" are made explicit by Vigo when Jean (Jean Dasté) dives underwater after being left by his wife Juliette (Dita Parlo) (Deleuze 1986, 79). There he begins swimming with and then embracing the image of his wife, enjoying a perception that he could not enjoy on land. The film expresses Vigo's own utopian hope that the perception of the workers, itself a type of rhythm involving balance and readjustment as they move about their barge, could offer a different view—Deleuze goes so far as to call them a different "race of men"—of human relations than the bourgeois exchanges on land.

In the Dardennes' documentaries, the Meuse had also given a new perception of space and time. Floating down the Meuse with Léon M. permitted us to glimpse the future and the past of Seraing, to reconsider the workers' community and its desires for a better society. At the same time, the jumpy camera suggested a seed of failure arising from the Meuse's passage through the industrial rubble. Over the course of the Dardennes' work, it is the latter tendency that has won out, as the Meuse has become more and more alienated from its promise. Absent from *La promesse* and *The Son*, the Meuse is replaced in *Rosetta* by the murky lake in which she nearly drowns. In *The Child* the Meuse is again, as in the memories from the Dardennes' childhood, a place of death, where people kill themselves or are killed. The scene itself was inspired by an actual news event that Jean-Pierre had read about, in which a fleeing mugger took refuge in the water while holding a tuft of grass that tore, sending him to his death. Stylistically as well, the Dardennes no longer explore the Meuse's possibilities through lyrical voiceover or creative editing and camerawork. The two thieves are shown from the water level, they lose their hold and dip under the surface, Bruno pops back out, carries Steve out on his shoulders, and that is all. For the viewer, the underwater is the darkest, most impenetrable *hors champ*. What happens there is a disaster that we cannot experience through the film, and whatever deep secrets Bruno might find out about himself under the waves are kept from our view.

The scene confirms what we have observed at the level of Bruno's relation to others since he carried Jimmy up the stairs of the abandoned apartment building. Bruno's body answers to others as if it had a mind of its own. He naturally knows how to hold the clinging baby, automatically picks Sonia up and seeks help for her, and instinctually struggles against the pull of the river to help Steve. Faced with gravity and death, Bruno struggles for life, for himself, and for others. Despite appearances, Bruno is not merely a self-adoring image, but a body that struggles to survive (figures 20–22).

Figures 20–22. Bruno discovers the ability to carry.

Bruno does not belong to the water; he belongs on land, which as Deleuze (1986) puts it, is more "tailored to solids," and where bodies have weight and encounter each other (81). Again the post-plunge-into-the-river scenes are filmed in slow sequence shots. Renier, who had studied mime and circus as a child, excels in these scenes that emphasize weight and fatigue. [8] His eyes are tired from sleeplessness, his skin rough and hair dirty from the plunge in the river. His soggy sweat jacket weighs him down. He disentangles the moped and begins a long, tired march through the city, pushing the moped as he had pushed the buggy. He leans against the bike, changing his step as he slowly falls into a lilting harmony with the moped, which wobbles rhythmically because of its flat tire. He first goes to Sonia's apartment, where he finds that she has left (or at least isn't answering the door), and then pushes the moped through the market and across the bridge of Ougrée (reproducing a shot of Igor from *La promesse*). The dénouement of the story shows how anticlimactic and impenetrably unsubjective the Dardennes can be. Bruno simply stops running and surrenders himself to the police station; the mid-shots of him at the station simply show him sitting, no longer in movement. Responsibility is shown as a simple relation to other bodies without any interior epiphany.

Another Dardenne film might have left Bruno here, at his solitary realization that he is indeed part of a greater whole. But *The Child* contains a kind of epilogue that underlines more forcibly than in earlier films the affective link of relation. The last *plan séquence* follows an ellipsis of perhaps a day or two. This shot itself begins by reproducing the film's alternating melody with a frame of Bruno alone, looking more peaceful, as he enters the visitors' room. He wears light gray pants and shirt over a white tee-shirt, looks rested, and his hair has been washed. The lines in his face are less deep and his skin looks clearer; he seems relieved of his burden. He sits and looks across the table at Sonia—who has come without Jimmy. Though they sit at the same table, the camera alternates from one face to another, leaving them in separate frames. Sonia asks Bruno whether he wants some coffee. As she stands up and moves away from the table (and the camera) across the room, she becomes one in the crowd of detainees and visitors; the camera even lingers on a frame of reconciliation in the room, the loving gesture of a father caressing his daughter's hair. It then discretely reframes on Bruno. When Sonia returns, it again pans from one face to another. Bruno asks how Jimmy is doing, using the child's name for the first time in the film. As in *La promesse,* Bruno's lies are here replaced with a different, responsible language, literally accepting his responsibility toward the other. The camera still does not frame them together, but his language seeks out a contact (figure 23).

Figure 23. Jean-Pierre Duret, Amaury Duquenne, Benoît Dervaux, Alain Marcoën (standing), Jérémie Renier, Déborah François (seated) filming the last scene of *The Child.* © Christine Plenus

Then, while making the simple gesture of drinking his coffee, Bruno begins to cry. The delicately wavering camera moves cautiously back and forth from his face to Sonia's as his emotion becomes contagious and she too cries. We then see Bruno take Sonia's hands and her crying intensifies. From the hands we move to their faces, finally together for the first time since Sonia threw him out. Alternation and absence have finally become togetherness. Again the brothers flirt with melodramatic cliché, but they escape it by avoiding runny makeup and indeed by the sheer physicality and durability of these tears that overwhelm them for several minutes. They engage in a dancelike embrace. Their foreheads butt, with their hands lovingly clutching the back of each other's head, a romantic gesture repeated from the scene at the car in the park (figure 24). Eventually through all the tears they show the outlines of smiles. As Luc writes, they cry "tears, tears, and more tears, and it's not sad" (L. Dardenne 2008, 163). Lightness and rhythmic balance is no longer in the Meuse, but in the tears that bring them together. The two occupy entirely and harmoniously the frame when the film ends.

Rhythm and tears both involve affective forces overpowering the body. Luc credits a book by the Levinasian philosopher Catherine Chalier (2003) for suggesting the idea of ending the film on tears, and for a similar sentiment of connection. In her *Traité des larmes,* Chalier examines various instances of uncontrollable crying in the Hebrew Bible and Midrash. Chalier explains that in Jewish sacred writings, far from expressing a negative sentiment, tears are often signs of a joyous return to a sense of place within a covenant. Creation, according to Chalier's reading, is imperfect—God himself cries over this imperfection—and its lack of wholeness leads humanity away from the feeling of divine presence, referred to as the Shekhinah, often interpreted as the feminine attributes of divinity that are associated with joy, beauty, and the inspiration of the psalms. The Shekhinah is located deep inside each individual, but it is exiled under layers of images or clothing, and if Bruno's leather has been replaced by simple clothing at the end of the film, it suggests that he has also shed his illusion of self-sufficiency. Dardenne writes that throughout all the moments of waiting, Bruno has been waiting for his own "loss of strength. Not a movement of a redemption or resurrection, but the rupture of a movement, an arrest, the lapse that allows him to see Sonia who is there, facing him . . . in tears" (L. Dardenne 2008, 181).

Figure 24. Jérémie Renier and Déborah François. |

Bruno's story is first and foremost a severe disruption so that he can reach "a point of goodness" inside, from which the tears flow (Chalier 2003, 172).

Tears remind the tearful one of his or her place in a transcendent relation. When tears are shed in the Old Testament, the covenant is felt again—Chalier (2003) explains that tears come when "pain is no longer condemned to itself" (164). They can therefore bring hope, because they imply a shared future, even if they express remorse. When Joseph cries at the sight of his brothers, he feels a return to a history of following the covenant. In *Falsch* we saw that Joe, a false Joseph, was unable to integrate a future; he is also unable to cry. Olivier's tears at the end of *The Son* are more hopeful, since they seem to indicate his return to life after years of mourning. *The Child* also ends by suggesting a more hopeful outlook. Near the end of his journal, Luc quotes the final passage of Chalier's book: "But when they discover the water of the morning dew, traditionally associated with awakening and the resurrection, do they not rejoice? This fragile happiness, this trembling before the hope of life, human tears, in their pure nudity, can sometimes make us feel them" (L. Dardenne 2008, 148). Tears are the opposite of cynicism or nihilism, for they offer hope for the future.

This is not a forgetful hope, and biblical tears do not offer complete solace. Chalier also describes a tearful Messiah, hidden away, according to the Midrash and the Zohar, in a secret corner of Eden, crying for the suffering of mankind. The Messiah cannot come out of Eden and enter history until this suffering, all this suffering in every individual from every generation, is taken into account. The Messiah, like Benjamin's angel of history, is a figure of remembering, outside the time of progress, looking back at an accumulation of disaster after disaster, too concerned to float effortlessly into the future. The Messiah's tears won't let the past pass by. Both Levinas and Benjamin, according to Chalier, suggest that the Messiah resides inside each person. In his theses on history, Benjamin speaks of each generation's "*weak* Messianic power" (Benjamin 1969, 254; italics in original). A strong or deep messianic power, which would necessarily be divine, would repair all the rifts and sufferings in history, turning history into a healthy unity. A weak messianic power means a responsibility not to forget, a "power to which the past has a claim" (Benjamin 1969, 254).

Returning to the last scene of *The Child,* we can see the marvelous suggestiveness of the *mise-en-scène,* the floating camera, and the gestures of the actors. Tears are first signs of Bruno's fallen armor, tears of guilt and repentance. Like Igor, Rosetta, Francis, and Lorna after him, Bruno emerges from a self-imposed solitude to his place in a group. The tears then inspire Sonia's tears, tears of compassion, forgiveness, and even love. Her emotion comes from an empathetic gaze, but also from a renewed bond that will lead to a future for the child. Together the two cry tears of reconciliation, tears that ratify their secular covenant, just as they move into the same frame and touch heads together. But unlike some melodrama, the tears do not expunge the shipwreck that Bruno has made of things. The resolution of the alternating musical rhythm of the camera in the last scene conveys this reconciliation to the viewer.

One might be tempted to reapply the label of "religious filmmakers" to the Dardennes (as Cardullo 2002 does in regard to *Rosetta).* But there is a unique kind of secularization of religion in their approach, which does not descend from on high but rises out of the quotidian *mise-en-scène.* In the journal Luc cites an illuminating passage from Jean-Paul Sartre. "When Pascal writes: 'the eternal silence of these infinite spaces frightens me,' he is speaking as a nonbeliever, not a believer. For if God exists, there is no silence, there is the harmony of the spheres. But if God doesn't exist, then yes, that silence is frightening because it is neither the nothingness of being nor Being illuminated by the gaze" (L. Dardenne 2008, 111). In a frightening world without a god, there is no cosmic harmony to inspire music or tears. But the citation continues: "It is the call of Being to man . . . *to see* is to pull Being from its ruin." Only mankind, through seeing and consciousness, can bring music to silence. Luc adds that it is the "infinite mission of the filmmaker" in particular to "make the world be, to make man be, by seeing him and making him see" (112). The music of the spheres, then, is first and foremost a human rather than a divine question, it is something produced by the practice of looking, recognizing, and making others see. For the Dardennes it is a question of locating a rhythm that organizes the images of a film: "the desire for a movement, of a line, is deeper than the imagination of images. Rhythm, breath, 'music' before images. . . . There is a rhythm, intensity, a tension that seeks its images and finds the shot" (113). If the Dardennes' second *palme d'or* is any indication, Bruno's tears also inspired the affect of its audience, made the rhythm between these characters perceptible, brought music out of the "silence" of Seraing and its Meuse.

Dans l'Obscurité

The Dardennes have themselves directly allegorized this affective transformation of the cinema space in a short film made in 2007. *Dans l'obscurité* (*In the Dark*) was part of an omnibus of some thirty films by various directors, called *Chacun son cinéma*, made to celebrate the sixtieth anniversary of the Cannes festival. The idea was conceived and produced by festival president Gilles Jacob, who asked each artist to make a three-minute film expressing "their state of mind of the moment as inspired by the motion picture theater, the communion room of cinephiles from around the world." Characteristically, the Dardennes' contribution deals directly with the social and ethical value of tears.

On one level, *Dans l'obscurité* plays out as an homage to Robert Bresson, an inspiration since their days at the collège Saint-Martin in Seraing. It begins with typical red titles on what seems like a black screen with a rich soundtrack of chanting crickets, presumably indicating the night of our title. We then hear a few gunshots, as hands suddenly appear on the screen, illuminated by a flickering light. We have seen these hands before, as they look exactly like those of Fontaine, the prisoner from Bresson's film *Un Condamné à mort s'est échappé* (*A Man Escaped*, 1957). As if to confirm the citation, the camera pans up to show the face of Jérémie Ségard, a band of light (coming from the film on the movie-house screen) crossing it like Fontaine's on the roof of his prison. An alert listener may also recognize the sounds of another Bresson film, *Au hasard Balthazar* (1966), which tells the story of an innocent donkey persecuted by its many owners until it is finally killed. The appearance of light in the theater is explained by the passage from night to day on the screen. One of these gunshots mortally wounds Balthazar. The last scene finds Balthazar, who at times is described as a simple animal but at others as a Christ figure, dying on a grassy hill, lovingly surrounded in death by gathering sheep, in an airy natural setting that recalls the maternal woods of *The Son*. We hear birds, the sheep's bells jingling, and dogs barking lazily at them. The sight of this longsuffering, innocent animal dying, surrounded by other innocent animals, has reduced many an audience member to sobs.

On screen, we watch, as so often in the Dardennes' work, a film of hands, here illuminated by the soft light of Bresson's film. Ségard makes his way down a row of seats (the film was shot at a liégeois art cinema) until he stops, reaches for a purse, and carefully opens its zipper (the close-up on the hand evoking a third Bresson film, *Pickpocket*). We hear a sniffle from his victim, whose bare arm we make out, as he quickly pulls back his hand. The camera follows the woman's arm up, and we see Émilie Dequenne's face, lit up by the film and bathed in tears at the very moment music begins to play—the simple and haunting theme of Schubert's Piano Sonata no. 20 that accompanies Balthazar's death. This image of Dequenne also echoes Godard's *Vivre sa vie* and its images of Anna Karina crying at scenes of Maria Falconetti, herself crying in Dreyer's *Passion of Joan of Arc,* quoted in many of the films of *Chacun son cinéma,* as if the movie theater were an obscure space of emotional contagion combining images, music, and silence.

The film does not end on affect, however, but on community. The tribute to the expressivity of hands continues. First shown in extreme close-up, Ségard's hands lead us into the film, through the theater. We are in the darkness of the cinema, but it is already a darkness illuminated by the film, infused with emotion, and inspiring a relation. Ségard's criminal intentions are offset by another set of hands, those of Dequenne, pushed on by the emotion inspired by the film. She reaches for her purse but touches Ségard instead. The camera lingers on the two actors' strangely interwoven hands, and then she lifts Ségard's hands to her lips and embraces them. The emotional power of the film touches the viewer, awakens her to a rhythm and overcomes her with an action related to a social consciousness. The Dardennes' allegory of the movie house literally frames the fraternal handshake that they have always sought in their work, mixing affect with touch and solidarity, transforming the theater into an ethically charged space.

Postscript: *Le Silence de Lorna*

The brothers' most recent film, *The Silence of Lorna,* was completed in May 2008 and was shown at the Cannes festival, where it won best screenplay. The film was released at the end of summer in Europe and on a few American screens in early summer 2009. Since the bulk of this book was finished in fall of 2008, I will only be able to deal superficially with this wonderful film now, in spring 2009, and without the aid of long discussions with colleagues and students. I have read the European reviews of the film, as well as the screenplay, and have been able to view the film very recently on DVD (I will refrain from exploring in depth the stylistic originalities of the film, including a setting in Liège and the use of a more stable, 35mm camera).

Many reviews of the film begin with this passage from *Au dos de nos images:*

> Perhaps our next film will be about a young woman who has every reason to be desperate and who continues to believe that everything is possible. A religious believer of sorts, even if God is dead. [. . .] How can a woman who doesn't believe in God believe everything is possible? Where does this crazy hope come from? She is strange, out-of-the-ordinary. A fictional character always swims against the tide (translation in Feuillère 2007).

We obviously find a number of Dardennian themes here: Lorna, played by the Albanian actress Arta Dobroshi, is a character built on the very Dardennian themes of despair, hope, and belief. But it is the strength of Lorna's belief, butting up against the impossible, that interests me here. To appreciate Lorna's folly, it is perhaps useful to at least begin by talking about how this film evokes issues I have discussed throughout this book.

The narrative kernel is in many ways typical of the Dardennes. Lorna is an Albanian who enters a "white wedding" scheme with a hardcore Belgian drug addict, Claudy (Jérémie Renier), so that she can gain Belgian citizenship. When Claudy dies—for he is expected to succumb to his habit at any moment—she has agreed to remarry, this time with a Russian. With the money made from this arrangement, she can finally realize her dream and buy a small snack shop in Liège with her true love, Sokol. Complications arise however when Claudy grows attached to Lorna and asks for help. During the first half of the film Lorna walks a fine line doing so, even making love with him once, while trying to maintain her dealings with the criminals running the marriage scam, led by Fabio (played again by Fabrizio Rongione). Fabio grows increasingly nervous, especially when Claudy actually manages to quit taking drugs. To get rid of this source of trouble, Fabio arranges the overdose that kills Claudy, whose death takes place in a striking ellipsis after which the viewer realizes only slowly that he has disappeared. The rest of the film, unfurling in a more varied rhythm, follows Lorna's reaction to Claudy's death. Her attachment to him is embodied, literally, in the child she carries after their one sexual encounter. The twist is that Lorna is not actually pregnant in any literal sense, at least not according to the medical examinations, and that her baby is a figment of her imagination.

The ethical situation is again expressed through circulations of money. The film begins with Lorna contentedly depositing money into the account that she and Sokol will use to purchase their snack bar. The scene could read like a Capraesque evocation of a modestly happy future for the couple, until we realize that it is Lorna who is actually at the service of the money, that she has sold herself into a scheme whose workings she cannot control. It is Claudy's decision to break free of addiction that stops up the flow of money, as is evidenced by the noteworthy detail of his own cash. He keeps it in a wrinkled brown envelope that he constantly forces on Lorna so that he won't be tempted to buy drugs, asking only for cigarette and food money. This is different money, money that nobody wants: Claudy because it would mean his death; Lorna because Claudy's refusal of money means that he has no investment in the scam working. But she agrees, and after Claudy does die, she begins to refuse the money that Fabio attempts to give her to pay for her trouble with Claudy. After Lorna scares away the Russian, Fabio and Sokol recoup their investment but leave Lorna with a mere 100 euros. But she has managed to salvage Claudy's cash, buried in its old envelope, and deposits it in a numbered account reserved for her unborn baby. After these intricate flows of currency we finally come to an ethical use of money that has in a sense been liberated and invested in more humane exchanges.

The human body reduced to its most physical state resurfaces in this film. Rail-thin, haggard, and bug-eyed, Jérémie Renier has undergone a major physical alteration for this role. Lorna's reaction to his character is first disgust, as she refuses to touch him or to let him lie under the covers of her bed. Claudy's withdrawal has put his body in a state of revolt: In one scene he doubles over in pain and Lorna places a bowl of water on the floor for him as if for a dog. Renier's emaciation makes such scenes quite convincing. This is the first time she helps him, but she is drawn into this relationship, again through touch: she carries him to the hospital when the pain is too strong and even struggles with him when he can't resist his urge for drugs.

Nowhere is their physical contact more intense and meaningful than in the remarkable scene in which Lorna and Claudy make love. The scene is beautifully choreographed, with Claudy chasing Lorna through the apartment to get his money to buy drugs from a dealer waiting downstairs. Lorna is able to break free, lock the door from the outside, and throw the key out the window. But Claudy is physically driven and suffering. In what seems like an act of pity, Lorna strips naked and walks to the entryway, where she has left Claudy, and the two embrace. Their busts fill the screen, behind them only the dim white surface of a wall. On one hand they seem like Adam and Eve, separated from the outside world, starting humanity anew. On the other hand they are not in a typical Eden. Their embrace is animallike: Renier's skeletal thinness emphasizes his vulnerability. Dobroshi also seems vulnerable, though she is a bit stronger and larger-looking than Renier. Their bodies resemble less the conventional pictorial images one has of Adam and Eve than the gaunt bodies of Jan Van Eyck's altarpiece at Ghent. Lorna/Eve steps out of her Paradise, the smooth running world in which she and Sokol would buy their snack bar with garden seating, into an encounter with a dying body in need of help.

This entryway links their embrace with another scene that transpires there after Claudy's death, and in which we surmise the extent of Lorna's difference and solitude. Two inspectors, one played by Olivier Gourmet, stop by Lorna's apartment with the results of the autopsy. Hovering in the entryway (with the camera in the same position as before), they evoke a telephone call that Claudy made to buy drugs the night that Lorna prevented him. When it is suggested that he tried to buy them because she had obtained a divorce, she begins to cry tears that the police take as a normal reaction to the loss of her husband. And yet, watching her in the same space where she had made love with Claudy and with the misinterpretation of the police, we recognize tears of guilt and responsibility. Such tears will, of course, lead directly to a relationship with the other as they had in *The Child.* They reveal an attachment that becomes over time a promise to a future. Lorna first misses her period, then has fainting spells, until finally she grows convinced that she is pregnant with Claudy's child. One could say that her responsibility creates the phantasm of her pregnancy. She alone has direct access to this experience and she fades away from our reasonable understanding.

Lorna's solitude grows more insistent and independent after Claudy's death. She is a foreigner in many ways, first as an Albanian living in Belgium, someone with a strong accent in French (Dobroshi did not speak any French before working on the project), the only important woman in the film (an "Eve" in the brothers' oeuvre), and even as an outsider invited into the Dardennes' family of actors (Gourmet, Rongione, Renier, Morgan Marinne). One of the most original narrative strategies of the film is the gradual stripping away of male characters that takes place after Claudy's death, eventually leaving Lorna alone with her baby. It is remarkable how quickly the brothers make Claudy fade away in our memory. Then the Russian backs out, then Sokol abandons her, Fabio dumps her on Spirou (Marinne), who drives her away from Liège on a deserted highway, likely in order to have her killed. At every stage Lorna's resistance becomes more determined, her silences and differences punctuate the fluid economy of the Dardennes' more stable images, until she is alone.

The film culminates in the kind of Sartrean silencing of the world that is not a turn to the music of the spheres but the call of Lorna's ethical being to define herself more freely. In the last images of the film Lorna slips away from Spirou's car and takes refuge in a fairytale forest, where the impossible new beginning with her child can take place, at least momentarily. The automobile noises disappear and we hear her footsteps on the crunchy winter leaves as Lorna collects firewood, the trill of a bird, and Lorna's words to her baby as she lies down to sleep in an abandoned cabin: "I let your father die, you will live. . . . Tomorrow we will look for food and water; we will find someone who will give." A rather cynical viewer might simply judge Lorna according to the biological facts and conclude that she is simply deluded, driven insane by her guilt. Another might read in her insanity—her "crazy hope"—a refusal to accept the given and an embrace of a new history, like Eve coming out of the garden with shame and hope. Perhaps Lorna is insane. Or perhaps this film cuts a crisis moment out of her life, which she will take up again the next day, perhaps with a more lucid (by our standards) hold on reality.

One major stylistic novelty calls our attention at the end of the film. As Lorna bids her child good night, we hear the first nondiegetical music in a Dardenne film since *Thinking of You:* the slow strains of Beethoven's *Piano Sonata #32*, chosen, according to Jean-Pierre Dardenne on the interview bonus feature of the DVD, for its combination of calm and tension. The music continues over the closing credits, giving the viewer a chance to "sit with Lorna" (according to Luc in the same interview) lest we feel too abruptly turned away. Rather than a violation of an unspoken Dardennian rule to forego all external music, this music is entirely in keeping with Lorna's momentary transcendence of the state of things.

Notes

1. Though exonerated of charges of treason during WWII, King Leopold had done nothing to encourage the resistance movement, especially strong in Wallonia. At war's end, he chose to live in Switzerland, until a referendum narrowly restored him to the crown in 1950. French-speaking Belgium had overwhelmingly voted against his return, and hundreds of thousands of demonstrators took to the streets. To end the impasse, Leopold abdicated in favor of his son, Baudouin I.

2. In *The Wild Child,* for instance, he helped Truffaut flesh out issues relating to paternity, while in Resnais's *Mon oncle d'Amérique* he helped adapt the thoughts of biologist Henri Laborit on aggression and human brain anatomy.

3. The case of Jean-Pierre Duret presents a good example of the Dardennes' long-term collaborations. Duret has worked with the brothers since their early documentaries (see filmography), but he has also worked with several well-known directors over the years, including Claude Chabrol and Dardenne favorite Maurice Pialat. His own documentary directing career has also gotten under way, in which he uses many of the same collaborative and ethical concepts put into practice with the Dardennes. Cameraman Benoît Dervaux has also directed a few films. And the entire film industry, small but active, of Liège owes much to the success and active support of the Dardennes (including their production initiatives in feature *and* documentary). Their actors, as well, have gone on to perform in an impressive array of films. In many ways their collaboration has had a direct if modest impact on the industry.

4. "To speak to make the world common, to create commonplaces. Language does not refer to the generality of concepts, but lays the foundations for a possession in common" (Levinas 1969, 76).

5. See also these lines from Levinas: "Conversation, from the very fact that it maintains the distance between me and the Other, the radical separation asserted in transcendence which prevents the reconstitution of totality, cannot renounce the egoism of its existence; but the very fact of being in a conversation consists in recognizing in the Other a right over this egoism, and hence in justifying oneself. Apology, in which the I at the same time asserts itself and inclines before the transcendent, belongs to the essence of conversation" (Levinas 1969, 40), and later: "Discourse is thus the experience of something absolutely foreign, a pure 'knowledge' or 'experience,' a traumatism of astonishment" (Levinas 1969, 73).

6. See also Levinas in such passages as this one: "Meaning is the face of the Other, and all recourse to words takes place already within the primordial face to face of language" (Levinas 1969, 206).

7. The Dardennes were not among the sixty-six signatories of the famous 1997 petition of film professionals in support of *sans-papiers* (only French directors were involved), but their films do work toward the *militantisme de proximité* (which Powrie glosses as "community politics," Powrie 1999, 15) of directors such as Robert Guédiguian and others.

8. For more on Renier and his working relationship with the Dardennes, see Emmanuèle Frois (2005).

Interview with Jean-Pierre and Luc Dardenne

"In the midst of things"

I leave the reader with a slightly abridged interview (translation mine) conducted in June 1999 by Bernard Benoliel and Serge Toubiana for *Les cahiers du cinéma,* after the release of *Rosetta.* In it, the brothers give a detailed description of how they work with actors and crew. They also provide a precious look at their approach to costumes, make-up, and some of the inventive technical *bricolage* that goes into their work. Its title sums up much about the brothers' approach. Chosen by the editors of *Les cahiers,* it comes from a phrase in the interview that typifies the brothers' frankness, and which in its literal sense has a slightly more vulgar ring in English than in French—"il faut être dans le cul des choses" or "We need to be in the backside of things."

Some of the commentary after your award at Cannes seemed to suggest that Rosetta *was not really a work of fiction. Do you still sometimes have the impression that you have somehow broken into the cinema clandestinely?*

LUC: Clandestinely, illegally, yes, without a doubt. After *Thinking of You*, we cut ourselves off completely; we no longer had the slightest urge to meet people in the profession or talk about film. From that moment on, I think we have been perceived as some sort of guerilla fighters. This allowed us to maintain distance, preserve our solitude, even if there are two of us. With *Rosetta* we felt like we were starting over from scratch, but we also felt more freedom. The problem is that the government commissions and some journalists like to stick a label on things: "The Dardennes equate social cinema." When we proposed the screenplay of *La promesse* we weren't sure it would be accepted. In the past we had made documentaries about the history of the workers' movement in our region, Wallonia, and here we came along with a subject that could have been perceived as "social," whence the misunderstanding. . . . On top of that we were asking for less money than most filmmakers would normally need.

You adopted a low profile . . .

LUC: That's right. With the strong critical success of *La promesse*, I guess they were thinking with *Rosetta* that "they have finally found their way, this is their thing." That's why we felt so much freedom. We took a risk and proposed a screenplay a little rawer and less polished, knowing that we'd rework it during the shoot. It was no longer completely clandestine. They went for it, "them" being the people with the money.

Rosetta shows a kind of radicalization in regard to La promesse; it is almost even rougher in its construction and its stylistic commitments. There is an ever-present notion of wanting to force things. From this point of view, the first scene is directly relevant.

LUC: Yes.

JEAN-PIERRE: We don't like the word "radical" very much.

LUC: Or then you need to clarify and explain—radical in comparison to what?

JEAN-PIERRE: We wanted to be simpler than in *La promesse,* in the screenplay and in how we shot the film. It seemed to us that in the *mise-en-scène* we were moving toward a greater simplicity.

LUC: In *La promesse,* we were filming a plot involving characters; here we are interested in gestures. It's more radical in that sense, more minimalist.

More "primitive art."

LUC: Yes. We tried to construct the film as if everything were linked by what happens to Rosetta, as she moves forward and tries to enter into society. In regard to the frame, there are many alternative possibilities that generate expectation for the viewer: "What is she going to do? How will she react?" We were counting solely on this to put in motion the desire of the viewer.

Above all else you were putting everything on Rosetta herself.

LUC: The actress went even further than we'd hoped. During the shoot, we saw that she truly made the frame exist, and we had confidence in her.

Did you write the screenplay based on a completely fictional character and then find an actress to incarnate Rosetta?

TOGETHER: Yes.

How did you meet Émilie Dequenne, the actress who plays Rosetta?

LUC: In the most mundane way, by taking out an ad in newspapers, and on the radio.

In a particular region, Liège for example, or in all of Belgium?

LUC: No, just in the francophone part. She needed to speak French, and without a Parisian accent, given that the dialogue was filled with "belgicisms," even more in the screenplay than in the film. We were also looking for a manner of speaking, an accent like our own, we who do not really speak like Parisians such as you. We received two thousand photos accompanied with letters, just as we had asked.

What age had you indicated?

LUC: Fifteen to seventeen years. We filtered them down to three hundred candidates, whom we filmed with a video camera. They would simply introduce themselves, and then we asked them if they have already done any theater, film, or video, even just with friends. They answer, and we then work through two scenes with each candidate. In the first one, we generally ask them to walk away from the camera, turn around, or eat something. In the second scene, there is usually a little more acting. This is the scene from the waffle stand, or more precisely, a mixture of many scenes. We say to each girl, "OK, you've just taken the spot of your friend, Riquet. He comes back and is going to ask you why you took his job." Some of the actresses begin talking a great deal, while others look on, holding back. Mostly our preference went toward the latter group. At the end there were five, then three, then two, then Émilie. With the final candidates, we worked a long time, played through a lot of scenes, some from the screenplay and some that we invented as we went along. Émilie won us over for two reasons. First, there was her gaze, a little teary-eyed as she acted, and her voice, which seduced us. Second, there was her interpretation of the waffle stand scene. She just started selling waffles, though all she had was a little table to work with.

She made the waffle stand exist.

LUC: The stand and everything else. I don't remember which one of us was acting with her, but we felt like we had just bought some waffles and we felt that it was really her stand.

JEAN-PIERRE: She gave herself completely, like Rosetta; she was perspiring . . .

LUC: When she finished, her mother, who was waiting outside, said to her: "What did they do to you?" She had arrived with high heels, a short skirt, and two or three sweaters. It wasn't winter, but it wasn't very warm outside. When she came in we asked her to take off her shoes because there was a rug and she was going to trip over it—she shrank ten centimeters. And then we asked her to take off the sweaters because it was warm. We could feel her panic rising. But slowly she vanquished it. She was covered in sweat when she left.

Had she read the screenplay?

LUC: Of course not. We also tried some fight scenes. We asked her to fight like a boy, and she understood immediately. She hits hard. She was like a little bull.

Had she ever acted before?

LUC: She had played *Madame Sans Gêne* [a play (1893) by Victorien Sardou and Émile Moreau, also subject of a Giordano opera, and a film starring Sophia Loren, about a beautiful young and free-spirited laundress who becomes a famous duchess in the court of Napoleon.] for her graduation exam. In high school she took courses in acting and declamation. We had to break some habits, but it did not take long.

JEAN-PIERRE: She was sixteen when she wrote us. She had just finished high school and had been accepted to the university. She still had a childish side to her. In her letter, which was accompanied by a few Polaroid snapshots, she told us what she was doing—a little acting academy, a little poetry—and ended by saying, "I want to leave theory behind and get to practice; I want to grow up among the greats. Émilie Dequenne." During our first meeting, she was walking toward the camera, with me off to the side. I asked her name, and she answered "Émilie Dequenne." I said, "My dear Émilie *Duquenne* . . ." But Duquenne is the name of the actor with Down syndrome who plays in *Le huitième jour* (The Eighth Day, 1996). She immediately told me, "No, no, that's D-E-Q-U-E-N-N-E." The story pursued her throughout the shoot. Already her name was something.

At what point did you give her the screenplay to read?

LUC: The last time she came, we told her that we hadn't made a choice because we still had one more person to see, and we gave her the screenplay. We were supposed to let her know within two weeks, before she left for summer vacation. But we weren't able to after all because we still needed more time for the other young woman. So we informed her father, and he called her on her vacation and took the screenplay for her. We set up the contract and all the necessary formalities with her parents, since she was still a minor. Once she had read the screenplay, we didn't even ask her if she had understood or not, we just began shooting.

JEAN-PIERRE: We never explain to the actors the whys and wherefores of the screenplay.

LUC: We told Émilie that we needed to work together for at least two months before shooting. Not every day, but practically. It was during this time that we worked on the movements and gestures of her fishing, the fights, making and selling waffles, et cetera. It was during that time that she became Rosetta. We also devoted a lot of time to choosing her clothes.

Did you help her choose costumes? Was it you who found the gray skirt and the boots?

LUC: We scouted in tandem with the costume designer, Monic Parelle. Émilie said, "I don't know anything about it, do with me what you want." She was right. She had a few hesitations and was wondering what we were turning her into. But it was essentially the costume designer and we who found her skirt, pants, and her ochre jacket.

What were your instructions on make-up?

LUC: She had none. All we did was dye her hair. In real life, Émilie is quite stylish. She had plucked eyebrows, which we asked her to let grow, et cetera.

JEAN-PIERRE: We had asked the costume designer to bring us skirts from Paris. We needed Rosetta to wear pants precisely when she could have been in a skirt, when she goes to Riquet's apartment. But we didn't want to totally transform her into a boy, which is why we thought she could wear a skirt through the rest of the film. On top of that, she had to be covered without being totally bundled up, since it was winter and she had to fight all the time. She had to be able to do battle while being dressed like a girl. The costume designer suggested several skirts, including the one in the film, which was one of a kind.

LUC: There were four other skirts like it, but not made from the same fabric. We had to wet the other skirts for them to have the same color. So during half the film she's acting in a wet skirt.

Rosetta knows how to do everything because she has a child's body, a boy's body, and a girl's body, all at the same time. But she doesn't know how to dance. When she dances, she has a sort of reluctance that handicaps her.

LUC: Émilie herself dances like a goddess. She would tell us: "How am I supposed to do that, I know how to dance!" She would have preferred that we change the scene.

JEAN-PIERRE: It's much better with Rosetta not knowing how to dance.

Finally, the most important part of your work as directors of actors concerns their gestures and movements: You worked with her on gestures until they were acquired, until she no longer thought of them, so that they became automatic.

LUC: That is what we wanted. Very quickly, when the gestures were acquired, she started finding things that surprised even us.

What you say about working the actor like a "model" until they become automatic translates a method close to that of Robert Bresson.

LUC: Before shooting, Jean-Pierre re-viewed a couple of Robert Bresson's films. I always watch the same one: *Un condamné à mort*. . . . Obviously, Bresson's films are important to us. In the screenplay, when the boss fires Rosetta to give his son a job, she circles around a mixing machine, turning it on while he keeps turning it off. Everything takes place around this switch. But on the set, chance arranged things because the switch wasn't working. We were wondering how to replace it. Rosetta is a girl who carries a lot of objects, heavy objects, and finally we thought of the bag of flour, which she had carried in the beginning and which represented her job. It was an idea we found while shooting. It was a good way of recycling this object, to use it otherwise, and she latches onto it as she had latched onto her job.

JEAN-PIERRE: The *mise-en-scène* focuses on gestures, gazes, and timing. Since Émilie is often filmed alone, in long takes, you need to establish a good timing so that the *mise-en-scène* works. We often found ourselves lying down on the ground so that we could give her cues.

LUC: We had set up an elaborate system, complete with batons that we would use to signal actors, telling them when to perform such and such an action. Since Émilie is alone in many scenes, she doesn't have references, no partners to cue her in on things. We would tell her to count to a given number, but we also needed to ensure that everyone was counting at the same rhythm, so we set up this system with the batons.

Some critics reproached Rosetta *for being an ultradocumentary film, too realistic, antifiction. And yet what you just explained about timing clearly proves there is a fictional writing, unfurling from the gestures of the character.*

LUC: It is a great pleasure to hear you say that.

When Rosetta stops at Riquet's to have dinner, the treatment of sound, the manner in which the direct sound is magnified, seems an attempt to unhinge reality.

LUC: We worked for two days on that scene alone, at the rhythm of one shot per day. At the beginning we didn't even have the timing down. We progressively found adequate duration and rhythm, but we spent a lot of time searching them out. It is direct sound that you hear. The sound engineer, Jean-Pierre Duret, would turn on the music and adjust the volume. We edited it as is.

In terms of sound, this is an incredible scene. They are sitting at the table, hardly even speaking. I was asking myself if the sounds of the utensils in the plates had been amplified during mixing, because it seems like the forks and knives fill the entire sound space of the shot.

LUC: No, we shot the scene just as you see it.

It really testifies to how uncomfortable they are. Everything is heard, since they don't speak.

LUC: That's it. I believe that during the mixing of this scene we added just a tiny ambiance, an airy background sound. This is a technological necessity when you work in Dolby SRD. It provides an ambiance, an inhabited silence. That's the only thing we added, just to allow for, technically, operating the digital version of Dolby SRD.

JEAN-PIERRE: The sound of the film is the sound of the shoot.

LUC: We reshot that scene thirteen times.

You filmed Rosetta emptying her beer in one gulp thirteen times?!

LUC: Yes, but it was alcohol-free beer (laughter). We reshot it with many variations. Riquet became more and more restrained, less and less chatty. We were groping toward the scene we finally wound up editing.

Like Igor in La promesse, *Riquet gets around on a moped. The object is like part of the character's body, we perceive it as identical to him.*

JEAN-PIERRE: Sound again plays an important role here. When he first arrives, even before we see him, we hear "vroom, vroom."

LUC: At first we had decided that Riquet shouldn't arrive as a surprise. He announces himself. He isn't someone who has plans or strategies; he's just there to help. He extends an open hand. In the first scenes, his presence is announced thanks to the sound of the moped. We modified the ending to have him come back with his moped to harass this girl who only wants to die. She announces that she won't be coming back to work because she just does things in a very ordered fashion. So she lets the boss know. Riquet comes to save her, but she doesn't know it yet.

In the last shot, which lasts a little more than five minutes, we hear the sound of the moped before we see it. Then the sound disappears. One wonders if it is just a moped passing by somewhere. The sound is both a promise and a source of incertitude.

LUC: Even more so, since once he shows up we don't know exactly what he will do.

Yes, but neither does he. In fact, you manage to strike a balance, to slalom between naturalism and realism. Your "realism" is totally doctored, reworked, and yet you avoid a naturalism reduced to a wretched view of the world. Your cinema seeks to force things.

JEAN-PIERRE: We have an expression—you can take it for what it's worth—but we always say this between ourselves: "You have to be in the backside of things." This expresses our way of working, everything that we've just described, meaning the timing, the jumping into scenes as they unfurl, the fact that we don't give characters a biography, et cetera.

Is that your expression or a Belgian expression?

JEAN-PIERRE: I don't know, but it is what enabled us to make *Rosetta.*

LUC: We are on the inside. We try not to illustrate.

JEAN-PIERRE: Otherwise you're just making kitschy prints, more or less well made reproductions, observations "on" things.

LUC: We have no point of view on the things we do, we are inside them.

Did you have a lot of raw film to edit?

LUC: The first rough cut was reduced from sixty hours of dailies into two and a half hours. At one point, we thought we wouldn't make an hour and a half. *Rosetta* lasted an hour twenty or an hour and fifteen minutes.

You didn't want the film to be any longer. You were aspiring to a blunt form.

LUC: The screenplay is ninety pages long, so that makes a minute per page.

JEAN-PIERRE: We were afraid the film wouldn't last even an hour and a quarter.

Let's get back to the mise-en-scène. *Does the camera follow the character, or does it, knowing where she will go, inscribe her in advance in the frame?*

LUC: Toward seven or seven-thirty in the morning, before the crew arrives, the two of us work through the scene with the actress. We imagine her movements. One of us plays cameraman, often with an auxiliary viewer, in search of the frame, while the other works with the actress. Together the three of us compose the shot. Then we call the camera operator, the sound engineer, and the director of photography (Benoît Dervaux, Jean-Pierre Duret, and Alain Marcoën). The director of photography watches, the soundman plots out the movements of the boom, and the cameraman brings along his equipment. All together we start looking again. The cameraman tests the feasibility of our proposals; we look and discuss together. Then one of the two of us stays with the actress while the other watches on a video monitor we often keep outside the shooting space, since there isn't enough room for it. The one who is watching the screen has a clear view of the frame. He cuts in most often, calling out things like "don't bother making that movement, it's better to let her move off screen; don't follow her; wait for her to come back." That's how we work. In fact, we have often both found ourselves in front of the monitor, because we presented a constant risk of stepping into the live area due to the actress's movements. We cut when the shot is finished. Then the two of us discuss whether we want to start again and change the camera movement. With *La promesse,* we realized that the frame would be defined by the body of the actor or actress. Before *La promesse,* even in our documentaries, which were actually very theatrical, the characters would show up in a preexisting space. Now we try to arrange things so that space is determined by that which fills it. It's a principal that we discovered late, and it has changed a great number of things. In this sense you could say that *La promesse* was our first film.

Speaking of framing, there is a scene, the one in which Rosetta falls into the water, that remains impressed on my mind. Rosetta's mother escapes from her gasp in such a way that the girl cannot avoid being shoved, and to my recollection the camera is unable to follow her; everything happens too quickly. Was that movement planned?

LUC: Yes. But there are two moments in the film where the camera movement was not at all planned. At the very end, after the argument with Riquet on the bridge, we pick up Rosetta closing the door of the trailer to leave for the morning. She goes to fill up her water bottle. The camera is in front of her, but suddenly the operator doesn't really know anymore where she is, and neither does she. Something happens, there is a blur and finally the camera lets her pass. We kept that scene.

JEAN-PIERRE: Everything happens so quickly, with such incredible speed, that even if we had planned everything, what actually takes place is always a little different.

LUC: Benoît Dervaux, our cameraman, was very intense, very on edge when we began.

JEAN-PIERRE: The cameraman is totally extracted from the reality of the set; he is *in* the film. He is just like her. He is wearing headphones, so he hears the sound from the boom microphones, just like us.

LUC: He's wearing different shoes, sometimes to keep the noise down, but also just so he can run. . . .

JEAN-PIERRE: Even if someone has just a little technical training, it can sometimes take control, especially on a shoot lasting eleven weeks, and people often fall into a routine. Sometimes we don't rehearse with actors, or else we do rehearse with them, but when the crew arrives on the set we film immediately, which always throws them into a panic. . . .

LUC: In the trailer, we had to keep moving the lighting, and the projectors were visible through the window. Two people were stationed on the roof of the trailer, holding pieces of wood with the projectors attached to the ends of them, moving them around as a function of the camera's movement. When Rosetta jumps out the window, the projectors were pulled away just before she arrives. So the lighting arrangement was extremely lightweight and mobile. Focusing was done from a distance, with a follow focus. The first assistant cameraman was a genius. He had surveyed all his measurements based on the cameraman, and not on the actress. He knew that when the cameraman was in a given spot, he had to focus in such and such a way, et cetera. He moved with him, and even if he didn't always do the same thing, he would adjust the focus according to the situation. Obviously he took advantage when he could see the actors and the cameraman at the same time; but otherwise he watched only the cameraman. He worked at a distance of between two to six meters. When we were entering and exiting the trailer, the DP also had a little slide for readjusting the diaphragm in an imperceptible way.

When you decide to shoot without preparation, it means that you accept the idea of wasting film.

JEAN-PIERRE: Yes. That is one reason why we shot on Super 16 and not on 35mm. It's half as expensive to rent the equipment and develop the film.

LUC: On top of that, the equipment is much lighter. We would have liked to film with Jean-Pierre Beauviala's new camera, but it wasn't ready yet.

I would like to know if you are aware of certain effects of the horror or fantastical genres in your film.

LUC: Rosetta is looking for a job. In the first scene of the film she punches a guy, and then spits in his face. On or off screen, there must be as many options as possible to make the viewer wonder "What is she going to do now?" These elements enable us to suggest that she could take off in a totally different direction. In *Rosetta,* these elements are constantly on the edge of the frame.

What did Émilie Dequenne bring to you on this idea of fear or risk?

JEAN-PIERRE: There came a moment when we felt that she was carrying the film, like she carries that bag of flour, or like she carries the jerrican. She was very good in the tryouts, but we were wondering how she could possibly handle nine months, which wound up being eleven months, during which she had to be there every day, get up at six-thirty, in winter and in the cold.

What did the awards at Cannes set off for you in Belgium?

LUC: All the women's press became interested in Émilie, who became queen for the day. Bells were rung, flags raised. In her village, which is basically a farming village, three hundred people gathered in the street, and the tractors with their shovels raised in the air. Everybody had put up banners proclaiming "long live Émilie" and "Thank you, Émilie."

JEAN-PIERRE: At the airport there were lots of people to see Émilie, including some from her village.

LUC: In Belgium there is also an old complex in regard to France. We have an infamous expression that goes "A thousand years under France." [In French "*sous France*" is homonymous with the word "*souffrance*" (suffering), translating to "a thousand years of suffering."] A lot of people, such as my bookseller for instance, would tell us, "We got them this time! They took the World Cup, but they didn't get the *Palme d'or!*" All the newspapers announced that it was the first time that Belgium had won. Cannes turned into a long combat of fifty-two years that had been won at last.

JEAN-PIERRE: The *Palme d'or* necessarily represents a victory against the French. There's no escaping it.

How did you react to the controversy that followed?

LUC: We didn't comprehend it immediately. And since we hadn't seen the other films, we didn't want to join in. That's not our job.

JEAN-PIERRE: It's not our place to make comments on the jury's choices.

I'm thinking more about what took place in the press.

JEAN-PIERRE: When we arrived at the press conference after the award, the polemics had already begun, but I had absolutely no clue it was going on. The first question was about the actors: "Why did you choose so-and-so?"

LUC: We explained to them that, for us, the issue was not whether Émilie was a professional or not, but that we were looking for unknown bodies, bodies that did not come from the history of cinema. We had barely gotten back at the airport in Belgium when we ran into people already up to date on the polemics, even much more informed than we were.

La promesse *and* Rosetta *focus on two characters, a boy and a girl, of about the same age. It seems as though the thing that animates your characters is their nascent desire. Rosetta seems to be tormented by her woman's body. She has her period, and we sense that she is tormented inside. Likewise, in* La promesse, *it is the gaze that Igor directs toward the young woman that leads him to break ranks with his father.*

LUC: Rosetta is a girl who is becoming hardened. There isn't a centimeter of space for anyone else. We compressed her to the maximum. She is on the point of exploding. Then a moment comes, it is true, when she cracks, and she begins to cry. One could call that desire. For the first time, one might think that she opens up a little space for another, even in her gaze. But until then . . .

For example, when Riquet is working in the waffle stand, the door is open a little and she watches him, as if through a viewer. She's watching because she wants to occupy his space, but she is also observing his body.

LUC: Yes, of course. That's very true.

The desire that inhabits these adolescent bodies that are being discovered for the first time—isn't this the driving element?

LUC: It's doubtlessly in great part for that reason that we chose protagonists of that age.

Someone made a comment to me that was very perceptive: Émilie's appearance resembles that of a modern Cinderella. She has a first name that, suddenly, brings to existence not youth, but a person.

LUC: That is why we gave her this name, which is also the film's title. She needed a first name. Any first name, but a name. So that she could be unique.

How did the idea come to you to give Rosetta such harsh menstrual pain, and to have her nurse herself as she does?

JEAN-PIERRE: You're the one who thinks it's menstrual, we have no idea.

LUC: It is true that one could interpret it like that, given what her mother says to her.

JEAN-PIERRE: When she talks to her mother, her mother says "When that happened to me . . ." But then Rosetta answers: "I'm not you!" The mother seems to be talking about her period.

LUC: There are times when it seems to be her period. But when she is fired, and she feels bad, and goes off in the forest like an animal, that's something else.

She is wounded.

LUC: She is wounded, in the literal sense, not metaphorically. Her anguish actually makes her physically ill. That also comes from us too, because we react in the same way. When we finished *Thinking of You,* not only were we unhappy, we were in debt. Jean-Pierre handled it in his way, and me, when I have money problems, I get ulcers, I suffer, I'm sick. After *Thinking of You,* it took us two years to get out of debt, and to recover from various physical ailments. It was terrible! When I tell you we hit bottom it's because it's true, even medically. When you owe millions to people and you have to sign statements of debt recognition against your personal salary, even though you have a modest salary like everyone else, it's distressing. The problem hounded us until we made *La promesse.*

Filmography

The first part of the filmography benefits from the work of Marc-Emmanuel Mélon and Emmanuel d'Autreppe, published in the *Revue belge du cinéma,* vol. 41 (Winter 1996–97, 2).

Documentaries and Early Fictions

Le chant du rossignol: Sept voix, sept visages de résistants. Une ville: Liège et sa banlieue. (*The Song of the Nightingale: Seven Voices, Seven Faces of Resistance Fighters. A City: Liège and Its Suburbs;* 1978)
Half-inch video
Only short passages of this badly damaged film have been recovered.

Lorsque le bateau de Léon M. descendit la Meuse pour la première fois (*When Léon M.'s Boat Descended the Meuse for the First Time;* 1979)
Production: Collectif Dérives, Belgian Ministry of French Culture
Direction: Jean-Pierre and Luc Dardenne
Photography: Jean-Pierre Dardenne
Image: Jean-Pierre Dardenne
Sound: Luc Dardenne
Black and white
40 minutes; half-inch video

Pour que la guerre s'achève, les murs devaient s'écrouler; Le journal (*For the War to End, the Walls Should Have Fallen;* or, *The Journal;* 1980)
Production: Collectif Dérives, RTBF (Belgian Television), Fleur Maigre coopérative
Direction: Jean-Pierre and Luc Dardenne
Screenplay: Jean-Pierre and Luc Dardenne
Photography: L. Ronday
Editing: E. Galopin
Sound: R. Joris

Mixing: G. Jodogne and L. Lambert
Black and white
50 minutes; U-matic video (low-band)

R. ne répond plus . . . (*R. No Longer Answers . . .* ;1981)
Production: Collectif Dérives, Centre Bruxellois de l'Audiovisuel, Mediaform
Direction: Jean-Pierre and Luc Dardenne
Screenplay: Jean-Pierre and Luc Dardenne
Photography: Stephane Gatti and Jean-Pierre Dardenne
Sound: Eddy Luyckx and Jean-Pierre Duret
Assistant director: René Begon
Color
52 minutes; U-matic video (low-band)

Leçons d'une université volante (*Lessons from a Flying University;* 1982)
Production: Collectif Dérives
Direction: Jean-Pierre and Luc Dardenne
Screenplay: Jean-Pierre and Luc Dardenne
Color and black and white
Five 7–10 minute episodes; broadcast video U-matic (high-band)

Regarde Jonathan: Jean Louvet, son œuvre/sa vie (*Look Jonathan! Jean Louvet, His Work/His Life;* 1983)
Production: Collectif Dérives, Wallonie Image Production, No-télé Tournai, Radio Télévision Belge Francophone, Ministry of the French Community of Belgium
Direction: Jean-Pierre and Luc Dardenne
Screenplay: Jean-Pierre and Luc Dardenne
Cinematography: Claude Mouriéras
Camera: Jean-Pierre Dardenne
Editing: G. Souphy, Jean-Pierre and Luc Dardenne
Sound: Jean-Pierre Duret
Assistant director: Eddy Luyckx
Color and black and white
57 minutes; broadcast video U-matic (high-band)

Falsch (1986)
Production: Collectif Dérives, Radio Télévision Belge Francophone (Liège), Théâtre de la place, Arcanal, Ministry of the French Community of Belgium
Direction: Jean-Pierre and Luc Dardenne
Screenplay: Jean-Pierre and Luc Dardenne, based on René Kalisky's play
Cinematography: Walter Vanden Ende

Camera: Yves Vandermeeren
Editing: Denise Vindevogel
Sound: Dominique Warnier
Cast: Bruno Cremer (Joe), Jacqueline Bollen (Lilli), Nicole Colchat (Mina), Christian Crahay (Gustav), Millie Dardenne (Bela), Bérangère Dautun (Rachel), John Dobrynine (Georg), André Lenaerts (Ruben), Christian Maillet (Jacob), Jean Mallamaci (Benjamin), Gisèle Oudart (Natalia), Marie-Rose Roland (Daniella), François Sikivie (Oscar)
Color
85 minutes; 35mm

Il court, il court le monde (1987)
Production: Collectif Dérives, Radio Télévision Belge Francophone, Ministry of the French Community of Belgium
Producer: Collectif Dérives, V. Marit
Direction: Jean-Pierre and Luc Dardenne
Screenplay: Jean-Pierre and Luc Dardenne
Cinematography: Alain Marcoën
Editing: Marie-Hélène Dozo
Sound: Thierry Dehalleux
Cast: John Dobrynine, Carmela Locantore, Christian Maillet, Pascale Tison, André Lenaerts, Jean-Paul Dermont, François Duisinx
Color
12 minutes; 35mm

Feature Fictions and Shorts

Je pense à vous (*Thinking of You;* 1992)
Production: Collectif Dérives, Favourite Films, Titane, Samsa Film, Radio Télévision Belge Francophone, Centre Bruxellois de l'Audiovisuel, Ministry of the French Community of Belgium
Producers: Dirk Impens and Jean-Luc Ormières
Direction: Jean-Pierre and Luc Dardenne
Screenplay: Jean Gruault, Jean-Pierre and Luc Dardenne, based on an initiative from Henri Storck
Cinematography: Y. Arvanitis
Sound: Jean-Pierre Duret
Original music: Wim Mertens
Cast: Robin Renucci (Fabrice), Fabienne Babe (Céline), Tolsty (Vladimir Kotliarov, Marek), Giles Lagay (Renzo), Pietro Pizzuti (Laurent)
Color
93 minutes; 35mm

La promesse (1996)
Production: Les Films du Fleuve, Touza Productions, Samsa Film, Touza Films Tunisia, Collectif Dérives, Radio Télévision Belge Francophone, Établissement de la Radiodiffusion Télévision Tunisienne, Centre du Cinéma et de l'Audiovisuel de la Communauté Française de Belgique
Producer: Luc Dardenne with Hassen Daldoul
Direction: Jean-Pierre and Luc Dardenne
Screenplay: Jean-Pierre and Luc Dardenne
Cinematography: Alain Marcoën
Camera: Benoît Dervaux
Editing: Marie-Hélène Dozo
Sound: Jean-Pierre Duret
Cast: Jérémie Renier (Igor), Olivier Gourmet (Roger), Assita Ouedraogo (Assita), Frédéric Bodson (the garage boss), Rasmane Ouedraogo (Hamidou), Hachemi Haddad (Nabil), Sophia Leboutte (Maria)
Color
93 minutes; 35mm

Rosetta (1999)
Production: Les Films du Fleuve, ARP Sélection, Canal+, CNC, Centre du Cinéma et de l'Audiovisuel de la Communauté française de Belgique, La Lanterne Nationale, La Régie Wallonne, Octobre Films, Radio Télévision Belge Francophone
Producers: Jean-Pierre and Luc Dardenne with Laurent Pétin and Michèle Pétin
Direction: Jean-Pierre and Luc Dardenne
Screenplay: Jean-Pierre and Luc Dardenne
Cinematography: Alain Marcoën
Camera: Benoît Dervaux, Amaury Duquenne
Editing: Marie-Hélène Dozo
Sound: Jean-Pierre Duret, Benoît De Clerck
Cast: Emilie Dequenne (Rosetta), Fabrizio Rongione (Riquet), Anne Yernaux (Mother), Olivier Gourmet (Boss), Bernard Marbaix (Campgrounds Manager), Frédéric Bodson (Head of Personnel), Florian Delain (Boss's son), Christiane Dorval (first saleswoman), Mireille Bailly (second saleswoman), Thomas Gollas (Mother's boyfriend), Léon Michaux (first policeman), Victor Marit (second policeman), Claire Tefnin (girl in locker room), Sophie Leboutte (fired woman)
Color
95 minutes; 16mm

Le fils (*The Son;* 2002)
Production: Les Films du Fleuve, Archipel 35, Radio Télévision Belge Francophone

Producers: Jean-Pierre and Luc Dardenne with Denis Freyd
Executive producer: Olivier Bronckart
Direction: Jean-Pierre and Luc Dardenne
Screenplay: Jean-Pierre and Luc Dardenne
Cinematography: Alain Marcoën
Camera: Benoît Dervaux, Amaury Duquenne
Editing: Marie-Hélène Dozo
Sound: Jean-Pierre Duret; Benoît de Clerck
Assistant director: Bernard Garant
Cast: Olivier Gourmet (Olivier), Morgan Marinne (Francis), Isabella Soupart (Magali), Nassim Hassaïni (Omar), Kevin Leroy (Raoul), Félicien Pitsaer (Steve), Rémy Renaud (Philippo), Annette Closset (Catherine), Fabian Marnette (Rino), Jimmy Deloof (Dany), Anne Gerard (Danny's mother)
Color
103 minutes; 16mm

L'enfant (*The Child;* 2005)
Production: Les Films du Fleuve, Archipel 35, Radio Télévision Belge Francophone, Scope Invest, ARTE France Cinéma
Producers: Jean-Pierre and Luc Dardenne with Denis Freyd
Executive producer: Olivier Bronckart
Direction: Jean-Pierre and Luc Dardenne
Screenplay: Jean-Pierre and Luc Dardenne
Cinematography: Alain Marcoën
Camera: Benoît Dervaux, Amaury Duquenne
Editing: Marie-Hélène Dozo
Sound: Jean-Pierre Duret, Benoît de Clerck
Assistant director: Bernard Garant
Cast: Jérémie Renier (Bruno), Déborah François (Sonia), Jérémie Ségard (Steve), Fabrizio Rongione (young criminal), Olivier Gourmet (plainclothes police officer), Anne Gérard (pawnshop keeper), Bernard Marbaix (pawnshop keeper), Jean-Claude Boniverd (plainclothes policeman), Frédéric Bodson (older criminal), Léon Michaux (police commissioner), Delphin Tomson (the girl with red hair), Stéphane Marsin (young man), Jimmy was played by seventeen babies.
Color
100 minutes; 16mm

Dans l'obscurité (*In the Dark;* 2007)
Producer: Jean-Pierre and Luc Dardenne
Executive producer: Olivier Bronckart
Direction: Jean-Pierre and Luc Dardenne
Screenplay: Jean-Pierre and Luc Dardenne

Cinematography: Alain Marcoën
Camera: Benoît Dervaux
Editing: Marie-Hélène Dozo
Sound: Benoît de Clerck
Cast: Emilie Dequenne ("Her"), Jérémie Ségard ("Him")
Color
3 minutes; 16mm

Le silence de Lorna (*The Silence of Lorna;* 2008)
Production: Les Films du Fleuve, Archipel 35, Lucky Red, Gemini Film, ARTE France Cinéma and ARTE Westdeutscher Rundfunk
Producers: Jean-Pierre and Luc Dardenne with Denis Freyd
Executive producer: Olivier Bronckart
Direction: Jean-Pierre and Luc Dardenne
Screenplay: Jean-Pierre and Luc Dardenne
Cinematography: Alain Marcoën
Camera: Benoît Dervaux, Amaury Duquenne
Editing: Marie-Hélène Dozo
Sound: Jean-Pierre Duret
Cast: Arta Dobroshi (Lorna), Jérémie Renier (Claudy Moreau), Fabrizio Rongione (Fabio), Alban Ukaj (Sokol), Morgan Marinne (Spirou), Olivier Gourmet (inspector), Anton Yakovlev (Andrei), Gigori Manukov (Kostia), Mireille Bailly (Monique Sobel)
Color
105 minutes; 35mm

Bibliography

Andrews, Geoff. 2006. "Luc and Jean-Pierre Dardenne." *Guardian* [London], Feb. 11. http://film.guardian.co.uk/film/2006/feb.11/features (accessed Dec. 25, 2007).

Aubenas, Jacqueline. 2005. "Les enfants de Seraing et les fils de Gatti." *Contre Bande* 14, 47–58.

Austin, Guy. 2004. "The Amateur Actors of Cannes 1999: A Shock to the (Star) System." *French Cultural Studies* 15, no. 3: 251–63.

Avon, Sophie. 2002. "Gourmet, l'homme droit." *Sud Ouest*, Oct. 23.

Baecque, Antoine de, and Serge Toubiana. 2001. *François Truffaut*. Paris: Gallimard.

Barthes, Roland. 1986. "The Death of the Author." In *The Rustle of Language*, trans. Richard Howard, 49–55. New York: Hill and Wang.

Bazin, André. 1967. *What Is Cinema?* Trans. Hugh Gray. Berkeley: Univ. of California Press.

Bégaudaud, François. 2005. "La matière, infiniment: *L'Enfant* de Luc et Jean-Pierre Dardenne." *Cahiers du cinéma* 605 (Oct.): 24–26.

Begon, René. 1977. Le Collectif Dérives. Une expérience de travail vidéo dans la banlieue industrielle de Liège. Thèse de licence, Université de Liège.

———. 1996–97. "Les années vidéo. Repères biographiques." *Revue belge du cinéma* 41 (Winter): 72–74.

Benjamin, Walter. 1969. "Theses of the Philosophy of History." In *Illuminations*, ed. Hannah Arendt, 253–64. New York: Schocken.

Brecht, Bertolt. 1964. "The Radio As an Apparatus of Communication." In *Brecht on Theater: The Development of an Aesthetic*, ed. and trans. John Willet, 51–53. New York: Hill and Wang.

Bresson, Robert. 1975. *Notes sur le cinématographe*. Paris: Gallimard.

Camhi, Leslie. 1999. "Soldier's Stories: A New Kind of War Film." *Village Voice*, Nov. 2. http://www.villagevoice.com/1999–11–02/film/soldiers-stories/ (accessed Feb. 10, 2007).

Cardullo, Bert. 2002. "Rosetta Stone: A Consideration of the Dardenne Brothers' *Rosetta*." *Journal of Religion and Film* 6, no. 1(Apr. 1): n.p.

Chalier, Catherine. 2003. *Traité des larmes. Fragilité de Dieu, fragilité de l'âme.* Paris: Albin Michel.

Chauvin, Jean-Sébastien. 2002. "Métaphysique chimie." *Cahiers du Cinéma* 572 (Oct.): 80–81.

Club des 13, Le. 2008. *Le milieu n'est plus un pont mais une faille. Rapport de synthèse.* Paris: Stock.

Contre Bande. 2005. "Conversation avec Jean-Pierre et Luc Dardenne." *Contre Bande* 14: 47–58.

Cooper, Sarah. 2007. "Moral Ethics: Reading Levinas with the Dardenne Brothers." *Film-Philosophy* 11, no. 2: 66–87.

Cummings, Doug. 2008. "The Brothers Dardenne: Responding to the Face of the Other." In *Faith and Spirituality in Masters of World Cinema,* ed. Kenneth R. Morefield, 91–103. Newcastle, UK: Cambridge Scholars.

D'Angelo, Mike. 1997. "Review of *La promesse.*" *The Man Who Viewed Too Much* [weblog], May 26. http://www.panix.com/~dangelo/col12.html#/apr.htm/ (accessed Apr. 10, 2008).

Dardenne, Jean-Pierre and Luc. 1996–97. "Au fil du fleuve." Interview by Marc-Emmanuel Mélon, Emmanuel d'Autreppe, Dimitri Coutiez, Nathalie Flamant, Anne-Françoise Lesuisse, Marc-Emmanuel Mélon, Thierry Stevart, and Geneviève Van Cauwenberge. *Revue belge du cinéma* 41 (Winter): 7–9.

———. 1999. *Scénarios: Rosetta suivi de La Promesse.* Paris: Cahiers du cinéma.

———. 2003. "Taking the Measure of Human Relationships." Interview by Joan M. and Dennis West. *Cinéaste* 28, no. 3 (Summer): 14–20.

———. 2004. "Cinéma à venir—en souvenir du jeune Pawel." *Positif* 505: 56–57.

———. 2005. Interview by Louis Héliot and Frédéric Sojcher. *Contre Bande* 14: 1–47.

———. 2008. Interview by Laure Adler. *L'avventura.* Radio France, France Culture, Aug. 27.

Dardenne, Luc. 2003. "Dans le dos de l'ange de l'histoire." Interview by Pascal Houba. *Multitudes* 11 (Jan.): 145–58.

———. 2008. *Au dos de nos images, 1991–2005. suivi de "le Fils," "l'Enfant," et "le Silence de Lorna" par Jean-Pierre et Luc Dardenne.* Paris: Seuil.

Dargis, Manohla. 2005. "Auteur Brothers Who Work like Cops." *New York Times,* sec. E, May 18, 1.

———. 2006. "Cashing in the Baby: The Dardennes on How We Live." *New York Times,* sec. E, Mar. 24, 1.

Deleuze, Gilles. 1986. *Cinema 1: The Movement-image.* Trans. Hugh Tomlinson and Barbara Habberjam. Minneapolis: Univ. of Minnesota Press.

Deprez, René. 1963. *La grande grève: décembre 1960—janvier 1961. ses origi-*

nes, son déroulement. Ses leçons. Brussels: Éditions de la fondation J. Jacquemotte.
Desimages. 2005. "Le cinéma des Dardenne I—Il a fallu rompre et repartir à zéro." (June 12). http://www.desimages.be/spip.php?article163 (accessed June 12, 2007).
Dubois, Jacques. 2006. "Conversation en Wallonie de Jean Louvet. Aphasie ouvrière et pouvoir du verbe." In *Les voix du peuple. XIXe et XXe siècles, ed.* Corinne Grenouillet and Eléonore Reverzy, 349–59. Strasbourg: Presses universitaires de Strasbourg.
Dubois, Philip, and Marc-Emmanuel Mélon. 1991. *La création vidéo en Belgique (1970–1990).* Paris: Points de repère.
Ebert, Roger. 2003. Review of *The Son,* by Luc and Jean-Pierre Dardenne. *Chicago Sun Times,* Feb. 21. http://rogerebert.suntimes.com/apps/pbcs.dll/article?AID=/20030221/REVIEWS/302210306/1023 (accessed June 6, 2007).
Eurofound. 1999. "Rosetta plan launched to boost youth employment." *EIROnline,* Sept. http://www.eurofound.europa.eu/eiro/1999/11/feature/be9911307f.htm (accessed Jan. 7, 2008).
Farge, Arlette. 2008. "Le cinéma est la langue maternelle du siècle." Interview by Antoine de Baecque. In *Feu sur le quartier general!* ed. Antoine de Baecque, 133–46. Paris: Cahiers du cinéma.
Feuillère, Anne. 2007. "Dardennes Take on *Le silence de Lorna.*" *Cineuropa,* Oct. 10. http://cineuropa.org/newsdetail.aspx?lang=en&documentID=80275 (accessed Nov. 15, 2007).
Frodon, Jean-Michel. 1996. "Le long chemin des frères Dardennes." *Le monde* [Paris], Oct. 17.
———. 1999a. "Jean-Pierre et Luc Dardenne, réalisateurs: Les films appartiennent à ceux qui les regardent." *Le monde* [Paris], culture sec., Sept. 29.
———. 1999b. "Un nouveau système de formes naît de la mobilité de l'outil." *Le monde* [Paris], culture sec., Sept. 29.
Frois, Emmanuèle. 2005. "Jérémie Renier, l'ami des frères: neuf ans après 'la Promesse' il est le héros de l'Enfant' de Jean-Pierre et Luc Dardenne, en compétition." *Le Figaro* [Paris], culture sec., May 17.
Frosh, Stephen. 2005. "Fragments of Jewish Identity." *American Imago* 62, no. 2: 179–91.
Fuller, Graham, ed. 1998. *Loach on Loach.* London: Faber and Faber.
Gatti, Stéphane. 1997. Portrait d'écrivain: Armand Gatti par Stéphane Gatti," on Armand Gatti, *L'enclos* (DVD). Paris: Doriane Films.
Girard, René. 1977. *Violence and the Sacred.* Baltimore: Johns Hopkins Univ. Press.
———. 1990. "Hamlet's Dull Revenge." In *Hamlet: Major Literary Characters,* ed. Harold Bloom, 166–85. New York: Chelsea House.

Guillevic. 1961. *Carnac.* Paris: Gallimard.
Hardt, Michael, and Antonio Negri. 2001. *Empire.* Cambridge, Mass.: Harvard Univ. Press.
Héliot, Louis. 2005. "L'Enfant ou De la Responsabilité." *Contre Bande* 14: 127–39.
Jobin, Thierry. 1999. "Cette môme guerrière prête à tuer pour devenir normale." *Le Temps*, culture sec., Sept. 29.
Kalisky, René. 1983. *Falsch.* Paris: Éditions Théâtre National de Chaillot.
Kehr, Dave. 2003. "Their Method Is to Push toward Moments of Truth." *New York Times*, arts sec., Jan. 5.
Kellner, Douglas. n.d. "Ernst Bloch, Utopia, and Ideology Critique." *Illuminations: The Critical Theory Website.* http://www.uta.edu/english/dab/illuminations/kell1.html (accessed Jan. 7, 2008).
Kierkegaard, Søren. 1983. *Fear and Trembling/Repetition.* Ed. and trans. Howard V. and Edna H. Hong. Princeton, N.J.: Princeton Univ. Press.
Knowles, Dorothy. 1989. *Armand Gatti in the Theatre: Wild Duck against the Wind.* London: Athlone Press.
Levinas, Emmanuel. 1969. *Totality and Infinity.* Trans. Alphonso Lingis. Pittsburgh: Duquesne Univ. Press.
———. 1996. *Proper Names.* Trans. Michael B. Smith. Stanford, Calif.: Stanford Univ. Press.
Limosin, Jean-Pierre. 2006. *Le home cinéma des frères Dardenne.* Paris: Doc.
Magny, Joël. 2005. *L'Aurore de Murnau.* Paris: Cahiers du cinéma.
Marks, Laura U. 2000. *The Skin of the Film: Intercultural Cinema, Embodiment, and the Senses.* Durham, N.C.: Duke Univ. Press.
Modiano, Patrick. 1968. *La place de l'étoile.* Paris: Gallimard.
Mosley, Philip. 2001. *Split Screen: Belgian Cinema and Cultural Identity.* Albany, N.Y.: SUNY Press.
———. 2002. "Anxiety, Memory, and Place in Belgian Cinema." *Yale French Studies* 102: 160–75.
M.S. 2005. "Solidarité . . . mon cul." *Le monde*, Nov. 27.
Neuville, Jean, and Jacques Yerna. 1990. *Le choc de l'hiver '60-'61. Les grèves contre la loi unique.* Brussels: Politique & Histoire.
O'Shaughnessy, Martin. 2004. "Suffering in Silence: Bodily Politics in Post-1995 French Film," *French Cultural Studies* 15: 219–33.
———. 2005. "Eloquent Fragments: French Fiction Film and Globalization." *French Politics, Culture, and Society* 23: 75–89.
———. 2008. "Ethics in the Ruins of Politics: The Dardenne Brothers." In *Five Directors: Auteurism from Assayas to Ozon*, ed. Kate Ince, 59–85. Manchester, UK: Manchester Univ. Press.
Piemme, Jean-Marie. 1996–97. "Usage de la blessure." *Revue belge du cinéma* 41 (Winter): 7–9.
Powrie, Phil. 1999. "Heritage, History, and 'New Realism': French Cinema in

the 1990s." *French Cinema in the 1990s: Continuity and Difference,* ed. Phil Powrie, 1–21. Oxford: Oxford Univ. Press.
Quaghebeur, Marc. 1984. Préface to *Théâtre. A bientôt Monsieur Lang et L'homme qui avait le soleil dans sa poche,* ed. Jean Louvet. Brussels: Labor.
Romney, Jonathan. 2006. "Weight of Water: Interview." *Sight & Sound* 4 (Apr.): 20.
Rousso, Henry. 1990. *Le syndrome de Vichy de 1944 à nos jours.* Paris: Seuil.
Schmitt, Olivier. 1999. "Radical." *Le monde* [Paris], May 25.
Séguret, Olivier. 2002. "Les multiples de deux; Ça reste à voir." *Libération* [Paris], cinema sec., Oct. 23.
Silvestri, Agnese. 2006. "Rene Kalisky et ses héros en mal de vivre." In *Entre aventures, syllogismes et confessions. Belgique, Roumanie, Suisse,* ed. Marc Quaghebeur and Laurent Rossion, 217–58. Brussels: Peter Lang.
Smith, Alison. 2005. *French Cinema in the 1970's: The Echoes of May.* Manchester, UK: Manchester Univ. Press.
Sojcher, Frédéric. 2005. "Les frères Dardenne: Une économie de la réalisation." *Contre Bande* 14: 155–76.
Sotinel, Thomas. 2002. "La légende dorée du menuisier miséricordieux." *Le monde,* culture sec., Oct. 23.
———. 2005. "L'instant perpetual de la misère moderne; *l'Enfant* de Jean-Pierre et Luc Dardenne." *Le monde,* culture sec., Oct. 19.
Stevart, Thierry. 1996–97. "Le devenir des mémoires brisées. D'une tentative deuce de réactualisation de la mémoire à la promesse d'un avenir." *Revue belge du cinéma* 41 (Winter): 35–41.
Strauss, Frédéric. 1992. "Portrait: Fabienne Babe." *Cahiers du cinéma* 461 (Nov.): 6–7.
Stroobants, Jean-Pierre. 2000. "La Belgique s'arme d'un plan Rosetta pour combattre le chômage des jeunes." *Le monde de l'économie,* Jan. 11.
———. 2005. "A Seraing, 'les frères' ont fait fusionner réalité et fiction." *Le monde* [Paris], culture sec., Oct. 19.
Tarr, Carrie. 1999. "Ethnicity and Identity in the *Cinéma de Banlieue.*" *French Cinema in the 1990s: Continuity and Difference,* ed. Phil Powrie, 172–84. Oxford: Oxford Univ. Press.
Teflin, François. 2005. "Les frères Dardenne: Tomber dans la Meuse pour changer." *Entrées libres* 1 (Sept.): 8–9.
Tesson, Charles. 2002. "À l'épreuve du cinéma." *Cahiers du cinéma* 572 (Oct.): 5.
Toles, Georges. 2001. *A House Made of Light: Essays on the Art of Film.* Detroit: Wayne State Univ. Press.
Virilio, Paul. 1991. *Aesthetics of Disappearance.* Cambridge, Mass.: MIT Press.
Waintrop, Édouard. 2003a. "En 2009, tout aura disparu. Jean-Pierre et Luc Dardenne à Seraing." *Libération,* special sec.: Un été 2003, Aug. 9.

———. 2003b. "Nous les appelions les bateaux fantômes." *Libération,* special sec.: Un été 2003, Aug. 9.
Williams, Alan. 1992. *The Republic of Images: A History of French Filmmaking.* Cambridge, Mass.: Harvard Univ. Press.
Wilson, Emma. 2003. *Cinema's Missing Children.* London: Wallflower Press.
Žižek, Slavoj. 2006. *The Pervert's Guide to Cinema.* London: Amoeba Film.

Index

Abraham and Isaac (biblical characters), xiv, 94–96
Akermann, Chantal, 43
Almadovar, Pedro, 83
Andrews, Geoff, 38
L'Arche de l'Adelin, 6, 7
Arendt, Hannah, 76
Astruc, Alexandre, 54
L'Atalante, 109

Babe, Fabienne, 39
Bacri, Jean-Pierre, 74
Barthes, Roland, xiv
Baudouin I, King of Belgium, 22
Bazin, André 61–62, 67
Beethoven, Ludwig Von, 123
Begon, René, 8
Belvaux, Rémy, 33
Benjamin, Walter, 13, 115
Benoliel, Bernard, 125
Berri, Claude, 74
Bertolucci, Bernardo, 5
Bloch, Ernst, 23–24
Boudu sauvé des eaux, 109
Breaking the Waves, 76
Bresson, Robert, 5, 39, 71, 79, 80, 117, 131
Brezhnev, Leonid, 18
Bulger, Jamie, 82, 85
Buñuel, Luis, 32

Cahiers du cinéma, 39
Cain (biblical character), 99
Caneele, Séverine, 66
Cannes, xv, 1, 65, 116–18
Capra, Frank, 102
Cassavetes, John, 71
C'est arrivé près de chez vous (Man Bites Dog), 33–34
Chabrol, Claude, 39, 123n3
Chacun son cinéma, 117
Chalier, Catherine, 114–16
Le Chant du rossignol, 10, 15
Chaplin, Charles, 73–76, 81
Chauvin, Jean-Sébastien, 98
Cheyenne Autumn, 71
Chibane, Malik, 44
Un Chien Andalou, 32
The Child (*L'enfant*), xiii, xiv, 63, 71, 101–17
City Lights, 73, 76, 77, 81
Clift, Montgomery, 107
Club des 13, 64
Cockerill, John, 2, 3
Coen, Joel and Ethan, 47
La Colonne Durutti, 6
Un Condamné à mort s'est échappé, 39, 117, 131
Coninx, Stijn, 43
Conversations in Wallonia, 21
Cooper, Sarah, 52, 62
Coppola, Francis Ford, 86
Crémer, Bruno, 30, 66
Cronos (mythological figure), 46, 54, 84

Daens, 43
D'angelo, Mike, 53
Dans l'obscurité, 117–18
Dardenne, Jean-Pierre, 70, 93, 98
Dardenne, Jean-Pierre and Luc: actors

(casting and direction of), 39–40, 65–69, 89, 128–30; as auteurs 42; automobiles (as recurring figure), 31, 92–94; camera technique, 21, 23, 31, 55–57, 65, 68–69, 87–88; childhood, 2–6; and the *cinéma de banlieue*, 44, 62; cinephilia, 71; collaboration (between them), 40; cruelty/cynicism 48, 52, 73, 79–80, 115, 122; dialogue/conversation 23, 28, 51–52, 78, 96–97; documentary career 7–23; editing, 54–57, 62, 103; Engis, 2, 8–9; ethics xii-xiii, 62, 72, 73, 76–77, 95–96, 98–99, 118, 120; film industry (position in) 34, 38–39, 41–42, 126–27; globalization (analysis of), 44–46; haptics 57–62; melodrama 38, 102, 108, 113, 116; the Meuse river (representations of), 2, 4, 8, 13, 20, 34, 102, 104, 108–11, 113; mission of filmmaker 116; off-screen space, xi-xii, 21, 27, 32, 45–47, 54, 68, 78, 81, 97, 106–7, 135, 137; production and funding methods, 41–43, 63–65; religion/secularization (themes of), xiii-xiv, 84, 94, 96, 100–101, 116, 119; revenge versus education/transmission (themes of), 83–87, 91–92, 98, 100–101; sensuous realism, 53–63; Seraing (relation to and representations of) 2, 4, 13, 22, 35, 36, 45, 63, 71, 103; tears (theme of), xiii, 75, 79–80, 99, 101,113–18, 121, 128; utopia/hope (themes of), 12–13, 22–24, 29–30, 53, 80–81,109, 115, 122; video, 7–17, 28; weight (representations of), 79, 107–11. *See also individual films*
Dardenne, Luc, ix, xii, 15, 31, 33
Dargis, Manohla, 104
Deleuze, Gilles, 109, 111
Denis, Claire, 92
Dequenne, Èmilie, 65–68, 74, 79–80, 118, 127–30, 138
Dérives (Collectif Dérives), 8, 10, 43
Dervaux, Benoît, 55, 87, 123 n3
Dickens, Charles, 104
Dies Irae: The Auschwitz Oratorio, 28
Dobroshi, Arta, 119, 122
Doherty, Paddy, 15
Au dos de nos images, xii, xiii, 40–44
Dozo, Marie-Hélène, 32, 42
Dreyer, Carl, 118
Dridri, Karim, 44
Dumont, Bruno, 66, 79, 83
Duquenne, Amaury, 55, 87
Duret, Jean-Pierre, 42, 49, 123n3, 132

Ebert, Roger, 85, 90
Egoyan, Atom, 83

Falconetti, Maria, 118
Falsch, xi, xii, xiv, 24–30, 38, 63, 65, 87, 108, 115
Farge, Arlette, x
Fargo, 47
Films du Carrosse, 64
Les Films du fleuve, 43
Ford, John, 71
François, Deborah, 108
Freud, Sigmund, 28, 29
Freyd, Denis, 63–64
Frodon, Jean-Michel, 68, 78
Frosh, Stephen, 28–29

Gatti, Armand, 5–7, 12, 15, 37, 42, 55
Gatti, Stéphane, 16
Germany Year Zero, 13, 45, 71
Gilou, Thomas, 44
Girard, René, 84
Godard, Jean-Luc, 5, 6, 37, 118
Gourmet, Olivier, 42, 45, 70, 82, 87–89
Gruault, Jean, 33, 37, 123n2
Guédiguian, Robert, 62, 124n7

Hamlet, 84
Haneke, Michael, 79, 80
Hardt, Michael, 44, 46
Au hasard Balthazar, 5, 39
Hawks, Howard, 107
Héliot, Louis, 54, 102
L'Homme qui avait le soleil dans sa poche, 22
The Housekeeper, 74

Il court il court le monde, 30–33, 34, 92, 104
It's a Wonderful Life, 102

Jacob (biblical character), 28
Jacob, Gilles, 117
Jarmusch, Jim, 92
Jaruzelski, Wojciech, 19
Jobin, Thierry, 70
Joseph (Old Testament character), xiv, 28, 115

Kalisky, René, 24, 29
Karina, Anna, 118
Karmitz, Marin, 6
Kassovitz, Mathieu, 44
Kehr, Dave, 83
Khruschev, Nikita, 18
Kiarostami, Abbas, 92–93
Kierkegaard, Søren, 94–95
The Killing of a Chinese Bookie, 71
Klee, Pau, 13
Kracauer, Siegrfied, 67

Labarre, Omer, 7
Lahaut, Julien, 22
La Louvière, 20
Leçons d'une université volante, 17–20
Leopold I, King of Begium, 123n1
Levinas, Emmanuel, xiii, 47, 51, 52, 73, 77, 81, 85, 96, 114, 115, 123n4, 124nn5–6
Loach, Ken, 39–40
Lorsque le bateau de Léon M descendit la Meuse pour la première fois, 11–15, 22
Louvet, Jonathan, 20–24

The Man Who Shot Liberty Valence, 71
Marcoën, Alain, 42, 55
Marinetti, Philippo, 32–33
Marinne, Morgan, 83, 89
Marks, Laura U., 49–50, 57–58
Mélon, Marc-Emmanuel, 10, 33
Mertens, Wim, 38
Michaux, Henri, 5
Michaux, Léon, 63
Minority Report, 83, 101
Misère au Borinage, 3
Modern Times, 76, 81
Modiano, Patrick, 24
Mon oncle d'Amérique, 37, 123n2
Moretti, Nanni, 83, 100
Mosley, Philip, 39
Mouchette, 5, 71–74, 79
Murnau, Friedrich, 102

Negri, Antonio, 44, 46
Night on Earth, 92
Nortier, Nadine, 71
Nous étions tous des noms d'arbre, 15

Oliver Twist, 104
Onkelinx, Laurette, 81
Ophuls, Marcel, 24
Ormières, Jean-Luc, 43
O'Shaughnessy, Martin, 10, 36, 39, 62
Oui . . . Mais, 74

Parelle, Monic, 130
The Passion of General Franco as Told by the Emigrants Themselves, 5
Penderecki, Krzysztof, 28
Pialat, Maurice, 123n3
Piemme, Jean-Marie, 11, 24
La Place de l'étoile, 24
Plenus, Christine, xiv
Poirier, Manuel, 62
Pour que la guerre s'achève, les murs devaient s'écrouler (Le journal), 11–15, 17, 22
Powrie, Phil, 44, 124
La Promesse, ix, x, xi, xii, 1, 2, 43, 44–63, 68, 71, 103, 112, 140
Psycho, 86

Quaghebeur, Marc, 22, 24

Radio Free Movement, 16–17
Ramsay, Lynne, 83
Red River, 107
Regarde Jonathan, 20–24, 31, 36
Reigl, Aloïs, 57
Renard, André, 3
Renier, Jérémie, 42, 45, 108, 111, 112, 119, 120–21, 124n8
Renoir, Jean, 62, 109
Renucci, Robin, 39
Resnais, Alain, 37, 123n2
Au revoir les enfants, 29

R . . . ne répond plus, 16–17
Rohmer, Eric, 39
Rongione, Fabrizio, 72, 74, 107, 120
Rosetta, xiii, 63, 65–82, 98, 100, 103, 125–40
Rossellini, Robert, 13, 45, 71
Rousso, Henri, 24

Sands, Bobby, 15
Sartre, Jean-Paul, xiii, 116, 122
Schmerling, Philippe-Charles, 2, 23
Schoenberg, Arnold, 27
Ségard, Jérémie, 117
Shyamalan, M. Night, 101
Signs, 101
Le Silence de Lorna, 1, 65, 98, 118–23
Sirk, Douglas, 102
The Son, xiv, 63, 70, 82–101, 103, 115, 117
The Son's Room, 100
The Sorrow and the Pity, 24
Sotinel, Thomas, 105
Spielberg, Steven, 83, 101
Storck, Henri, 33
Strauss, Richard, 25, 27
Sunrise, 102

Ten, 92–93
Tesson, Charles, 101
Thinking of You, xi, xii, xiv, 31, 33–40, 42, 43, 53, 123, 140
Toles, George, 67, 79, 80
Toto le héros, 24, 33
Toubiana, Serge, 125
The Train of the Good God, 21, 22
Tréfois, Paul, 10
Truffaut, François, 5, 37, 42, 64, 123n2

Vanden Ende, Walter, 24
Van der Keuken, Johan, 43, 67–68, 104
Van Dormael, Jaco, 24
Van Eyck, Jan, 121
Vendredi soir, 92
Vigo, Jean, 109
Vilar, Jean, 5
Virilio, Paul, 31, 32
Vivre sa vie, 118
Von Trier, Lars, 71, 76

Wallonia, xiii, 3, 4, 20
Watson, Emily, 76
Wayne, John, 107
The Wild Child, 123n2
Williams, Alan, 54
Wilson, Emma, 83

Žižek, Slavoj, 86
Zoncka, Erick, 62

Books in the series
Contemporary Film Directors

Nelson Pereira dos Santos
Darlene J. Sadlier

Abbas Kiarostami
Mehrnaz Saeed-Vafa and Jonathan Rosenbaum

Joel and Ethan Coen
R. Barton Palmer

Claire Denis
Judith Mayne

Wong Kar-wai
Peter Brunette

Edward Yang
John Anderson

Pedro Almodóvar
Marvin D'Lugo

Chris Marker
Nora Alter

Abel Ferrara
Nicole Brenez, translated by Adrian Martin

Jane Campion
Kathleen McHugh

Jim Jarmusch
Juan Suárez

Roman Polanski
James Morrison

Manoel de Oliveira
John Randal Johnson

Neil Jordan
Maria Pramaggiore

Paul Schrader
George Kouvaros

Jean-Pierre Jeunet
Elizabeth Ezra

Terrence Malick
Lloyd Michaels

Sally Potter
Catherine Fowler

Atom Egoyan
Emma Wilson

Albert Maysles
Joe McElhaney

Jerry Lewis
Chris Fujiwara

Jean-Pierre and Luc Dardenne
Joseph Mai

Joseph Mai is an assistant professor
of French at Clemson University.

The University of Illinois Press
is a founding member of the
Association of American University Presses.

Composed in 10/13 New Caledonia LT Std
with Helvetica Neue LT Std display
by Barbara Evans
at the University of Illinois Press
Manufactured by Thomson-Shore, Inc.

University of Illinois Press
1325 South Oak Street
Champaign, IL 61820-6903
www.press.uillinois.edu